JAN   1992

799.26
Cap   Capstick, Peter
         Hathaway

         Sands of silence

DUE DATE

SANDS *of* SILENCE

BY THE SAME AUTHOR

Death in the Long Grass
Death in the Silent Places
Death in the Dark Continent
Safari: The Last Adventure
Peter Capstick's Africa: A Return to the Long Grass
The Last Ivory Hunter: The Saga of Wally Johnson
Maneaters
Last Horizons: Hunting, Fishing, and Shooting on Five Continents
Death in a Lonely Land: More Hunting, Fishing, and Shooting on Five Continents

THE PETER CAPSTICK LIBRARY

Peter Capstick, Series Editor

The Man-Eaters of Tsavo Lt. Col. J. H. Patterson, D.S.O.
Hunting the Elephant in Africa Capt. C. H. Stigand
African Hunter Baron Bror von Blixen-Finecke
The Book of the Lion Sir Alfred E. Pease
Big Game Hunting in North-Eastern Rhodesia Owen Letcher
Memories of an African Hunter Denis D. Lyell
African Game Trails Theodore Roosevelt
African Adventure Denis D. Lyell
Big Game Hunting in Central Africa William Buckley
Kill: or Be Killed Major W. Robert Foran
After Big Game in Central Africa Edouard Foà
Big Game Hunting and Collecting in East Africa, 1903–1926 Kálmán Kittenberger
The Recollections of William Finaughty: Elephant Hunter 1864–1875 William Finaughty
Lion-Hunting in Somali-land Captain C. J. Melliss

SANDS *of* SILENCE

ON SAFARI IN NAMIBIA

PETER HATHAWAY CAPSTICK

ST. MARTIN'S PRESS

NEW YORK

SANDS OF SILENCE. Copyright © 1991 by Peter Hathaway Capstick. All rights reserved. Printed in the United States of America. No part of this book may be used or reproduced in any manner whatsoever without written permission except in the case of brief quotations embodied in critical articles or reviews. For information, address St. Martin's Press, 175 Fifth Avenue, New York, N.Y. 10010.

Design by Robert Bull Design

Library of Congress Cataloging-in-Publication Data

Capstick, Peter Hathaway.
    Sands of silence : on safari in Namibia / Peter Hathaway Capstick.
      p.   cm.
    ISBN 0-312-06459-4
    1. Big game hunting—Namibia.   2. Safaris—Namibia. I. Title.
SK255.N35C37   1991
799.2'6'096881—dc20   91-21808
                                                  CIP

First Edition: October 1991

10 9 8 7 6 5 4 3 2 1

With warm regards to my old Botswana safari friends,
Dr. Bruce L. Melrose and professional hunter George Hoffman,
both sportsmen and hunters worthy of the title.

"The essence of elephant-hunting is discomfort in such lavish proportions that only the wealthy can afford it."

—Beryl Markham,
West with the Night

FOREWORD

I had never heard of Bushmanland before that afternoon at the bar of a resort and casino where Fiona and I were attending the South African Professional Hunters Association annual meeting.

As we squinted through the warm November sunshine above the decorative pools, Fiona noticed that Volker and Anke Grellmann were already there, a couple of cold, sweat-beaded Lion Lagers already in hand. I already had a feeling that an adventure was beginning.

I had known Volker and his wife, Anke, for a couple of years now, and was aware of the German-born hunter's growing reputation in what was then South-West Africa, due to become Namibia the following year, in 1989. It was first-class. Volker stood up and took my hand, his impressive height and gray-streaked beard making me feel oddly like a small boy being led to the bathroom. I ordered a couple of somethings from a fleeting waitress, and Fifi and I sat down across from Anke, who was svelte and well-tanned as usual.

I had asked Volker, on one of my sudden, extremely rare insights of brilliance, to give some thought to our coming up to Namibia to take my first elephant the safari season after the rains, maybe late, possibly the last slot in his bookings. As he knew, I had never taken a jumbo for myself, although I had been a control or cropping officer in Zambia and elsewhere, and had shot about eight hundred for the governments some twenty years ago. Coupled with my years as a professional hunter, I had probably taken thirty or so more, although they always belonged to safari clients. If we made a deal, finally I would have my own license. To enter terminal meditation without having taken my own elephant after so many years seemed unreasonable anyway.

The more I thought about it over the several hours before our meeting that late afternoon, maybe I would be able to swat a couple of birds with a single stick. Ken Wilson, president of Sportsmen on Film, the Hollywood production company with whom I had done four award-winning videos, had been after me to fill out our offerings with elephant and leopard. Who knew? Maybe there was a book in it. It would be nothing short of personal perfidy if I didn't at least discuss the matter, I told a shyly grinning Fifi. After all, there would be several projects as well as, I hoped, a nice pair of tusks that would go ever so handsomely in her new house. After the application of considerably more logic, I had collared Volker and set up the date.

"So, what are the chances of getting booked next year?" I asked him.

He took a long drink of his beer and glanced at Anke. "Well, are you aware that we are working on an application basis?" I wondered why Volker rarely if ever advertised. He didn't have to. I answered that I was not aware, and how many applications did he have?

"Sixty for ten elephants. Mostly Europeans, Germans and such." My face fell. "I'll tell you, too, that they are cutting each other's throats for a chance at Bushmanland," he said in his whisper of a German accent. A long silence sank like wet fog into the tablecloth. "However," said Volker with a solid grin, "I just have a feeling that if you were to apply, you just might—might, I say—be accepted."

I didn't know who was more toothy—Fifi, me, Volker, or Anke.

We sat together until long after darkness had slid like silent silk from beyond the dead volcanoes of Bophuthatswana, the Tswana homeland, and finally had to light the candle between us. By the time we were talked out, I found that this had been Volker's first year with Anvo Safaris, a company he started years ago, in a new concession area that covered all of Bushmanland. "Where?" I asked.

"Bushmanland. You know, an old Africa hand like you! The

area given to the !Kung Bushmen offshoot, the Ju/Wasi." I didn't know, old Africa hand or not. "We got the concession this year for three seasons. Nothing, and I mean nothing, but bull elephants. No cows. No calves. They're up in the Kaudom, the game reserve. Only old boys there. Sort of a geriatric home. Of course, there's been nothing written about it, as I wanted the first season to see what would happen. Maybe it would be a bust. It wasn't."

When Volker arrived in Bushmanland from Windhoek, the capital of South-West/Namibia, he could hardly get around for a look, what with all the water. The great Nai-Nai Pan or catchment had expanded into a trial-sized ocean, and years of semi-dormant bush choked everything with new life from the heavy rains of 1987, the year that broke the almost-decade-long drought. When it came to selecting the area that would be his exclusive domain for leading hunting expeditions—his concession—Volker had a choice, either the Caprivi Strip, a tendril of land to the northeast across from the northern Botswana border, or Bushmanland, segregated from the rest of the country's tribal areas in 1976. Directly north of Bushmanland is Kavango, and south is Hereroland. East is Botswana. Oh, *now* you know where we are talking about.

Yet, despite the remoteness of Bushmanland, Volker and Anke chose the area. They were fascinated by the few people who live in this northern Kalahari Desert land, the Bushmen themselves.

Bushmanland is the home of the Ju/Wasi or Ju/Wa, who form part of the !Kung, whose name is pronounced by a ferocious dental clack plus a sound that is a fairly reasonable facsimile of the spelling seen here. I had spent some time while a professional hunter in Botswana with the Central Kalahari tribes of Bushmen. But they were considerably more tame than the !Kung, although in a year or so the Bushmanland people have all but forsaken their traditional dress of loincloth, headdress and a prayer, for dirty and stained white man's handouts. But more of that later. When Volker and Anke first went there in 1987, and for some of the season of 1988, there were still men who wore traditional dress, at least when hunting. But most of that is gone now that they have received political T-shirts and an almost endless supply of booze for their votes in elections.

Bushmanland is a small territory in a very big country, but the home of the Ju/Wasi is as big as Hawaii. Even on visiting days one would be hard put to scrounge up more than two thousand souls. Nobody knows where these small people come from, but it is generally agreed that they are the surviving prototype of the oldest people in Africa, their tenure in that continent being at least thirty thousand years old. They are neither Negroid nor Mongoloid, despite their epicanthic eye-folds and "spot" near the base of the spine at birth. To save you thousands of pages of research, they can be traced back through paleontological layering at least to a time that would make them the contemporaries of the people who did such fine painting at Altamira in Spain, although the modern Bushmen insist that they did no rock carving or painting to their knowledge. Actually, the first reference we have on Bushmen is from Sofala, in today's Mozambique, by an Arab historian in about A.D. 1000. They have been steadily driven from their lands to the depths of the deserts, where nobody else can survive, certainly not the black or white pastoralists who have persecuted them, sometimes with reason and sometimes without. Today, too late and far too little, there is an indignation that seems to have taken root among the more "civilized" nations at even the use of the word "Bushman," the name somehow being interpreted as demeaning. Certainly, this is ridiculous. After all, despite many mixings of genes with other peoples, especially blacks, there is no implication of sneer other than in the ear of the listener to call them Bushmen and not the more in-fashion "San." Japan has gone to the extent of deleting from all school textbooks the term "Bushman," substituting "San" through some bleary sense of racial righteousness. I wonder if they will change the name of their own aboriginal people, the Ainu, too?

Certainly I do not use the word "Bushman" in even the most remotely negative sense.

I hardly slept that night at the Cascades Hotel in Sun City, cursing myself for questions I had not asked Volker and Anke. But, as usual, tomorrow took care of itself. I find it wryly interesting that all authors, safari-booking agents and other riffraff are given free safaris for the wonderful exposure the safari company will receive later. Personally, and I can cite other examples, I don't work this way. If I accept too much charity, I am not free to write about a trip or a hunt the way it really happened. Too many lawns to water. Thus, after my evening with Volker Grellmann and his wife, I spent a day on the telephone, making deals for a new video with Ken Wilson in California (who never sleeps, anyway) as well as spreading some electronic imagery among the faithful at St. Martin's Press, Inc. By the time I had gotten together with Volker and Anke again, I had forgotten what I was going to ask them anyway. So I wrote out the deposit check.

Given that a foreword is supposed to prepare the reader for the main part of the book, I can't think of any more clever place to put a list of *dramatis personae* than here. You will find most of their names mentioned in the Acknowledgments, but I have to start somewhere.

The first is M. Philip Kahl, Ph.D., with whom I have worked on articles since 1970 and books since 1977. Phil is probably the finest wildlife photographer around anywhere, as his work in this book shows. He recently won a MacArthur Fellowship, which is unique in that it gives him something around a third of a million dollars over about five years to do whatever he wants to do! He does not have to publish or even work to get the money like clockwork, just open the envelopes. If there is anybody who should have been born in Africa, it's Phil. He has lived for five years in Kenya, and has tackled such problems as designing mudskis for high-altitude Bolivian swamps. He has photographed storks in Poland, and has been a lecturer on trips to the Antarctic. Probably the reigning expert on wading birds, especially storks, Phil agreed to come on our six weeks in South-West/Namibia together for no more than his air fare and expenses. That's the sort of deal that even I can accept! Phil has written for and done many covers for *National Geographic, International Wildlife, Audubon* and other magazines of similar caliber. We also tend to get along.

Jerry and Bam Heiner are close pals who happened to be on safari with Volker's company, Anvo Safaris, just before I hunted myself. Also friends and neighbors of Ken Wilson of Sportsmen on Film, they were so kind as not only to keep me company but to allow us to film their hunt. Jerry took a better elephant than I did—an eighty-four pounder—and got a fine male leopard besides. Of course, I hate him. . . .

I have told you—and will tell you more—about Anke and Volker themselves, but their staff certainly should be included here. First were a couple, Doug and Angi Stephensen, Doug being a professional hunter working for Volker and Angi, running the Klein Dobe Camp—as it was called after the then-dry pan nearby—for Anvo. Angi is a superb cook and Doug a fine and experienced hunter who went far beyond the call of duty to get me a leopard worth filming. That Doug got his client, Hanley Sayers, a ninety-four-pound-per-side elephant was an example of his expertise and professionalism. Both Doug and Angi are good at what they do, and at putting up with me around six weeks of campfires. Doug was born in the then Northern Rhodesia and learned his trade from the well-known Andrew MacLagen. Angi is German. Where she learned to cook is not known, but wherever it was I'm certain that she is missed.

Hanley Sayers is what you hope will get off the plane when you meet your client for the next safari. An ex–fighter pilot from Tennessee, he actually looked like a jet-fighter man turned elephant hunter. Hanley had been rained out in May of the same year when all elephants left the concession area because of late rains well into the dry season. He had rebooked and spent much of his time in the bush with Doug for a second hunt, yet had emerged hardly the worse for the experience. He was, naturally, inhibited during his hunt by his relative abstinence and clear eyes (elephants can spot a clear eye a long way away), and though I am sure Doug and Hanley's video man, Glen Lambrecht, tried to set an example for camouflaged eyes, Hanley was hopeless.

Hanley had a .500/.465 double rifle that was the epitome of good taste. Made by a famous British firm, it was just post–World War I. Despite his obvious shortcomings of early rising and hard hunting, I must say that he shot it in good taste, too.

Arnold Huber was sort of Volker's adjustable spanner, as the British would say, lending a most competent hand to any endeavor, whether it was elephant hunting, getting together a bunch of Bushmen for the video man, or catching puff adders and then handling them. For sure, he will be bitten one of these days, since a puff adder (*Bitis arietans*) is among the most dangerous of all snakes to fool with. He was invaluable in doing various things to set up scenes for the camera, and will make a fine professional hunter when he finishes his apprenticeship with Volker. By the time we left, his Ju/Wa language wasn't all that bad either. The Bushmen knew and trusted Arnie, and he deserved their trust.

Volker's hunting staff and Anke's camp cooks and waiters were excellent. Everything was well in hand when Johnny and Jonas, Ovambo tribesmen, took up a spoor. Both had been with Volker for years. Johnny was badly shot up by mistake while going home from a wedding after what is presumed to have been more than a couple. Security forces opened up on his car after he didn't stop when ordered. But he seemed to take the blame on himself. In any case, he has recovered over these several years and is a grand tracker. Jonas is not only a fine tracker in his own right, but is one of the finest-looking men I have seen in Africa. In Hollywood, he would knock 'em into the aisles!

Volker had one Bushman tracker who spoke considerable Afrikaans, but I never did hunt with Petrus (his adopted name, as the original was too difficult) the whole time I was there. Perhaps he was overserved booze by vote-hungry ex-terrorists too often, I don't know.

I hate lines like "last but not least," but it looks as if I am stuck with it to bring in Roger Olkowski. I must say that his and my ideas of cinematographic entertainment somewhat differed, as he had done a lot of work on low-budget films, but he was always working on recalcitrant equipment and lenses and learning constantly. From California, he had never seen a wild elephant before coming on this safari; in fact, he arrived with Jerry and Bam Heiner considerably earlier than Phil and I. I suspect I have to tell no reader that working in the depths of Bushmanland is a bit different from working in Hollywood, and at first, Roger had his problems with devil-possessed cameras and demon microphones. Yet he stuck with it and delivered excellent work. What made his work doubly difficult was that we had to work *around* him or we would have had no videotape. Not a move could be made without being certain that Roger had a proper angle on the doings. He had no gaffers or the multitude of thousands we now see on the credits of films and videos. He did it all himself. And he did it well. A young man, maybe thirty at the outside, he was always there, every day picking up more of the safari life.

AUTHOR'S NOTE

The various Bushmen languages vary substantially from one another, but are common to an untrained ear for their "clicks," of which there are a great many types. These are commonly expressed in Roman script by various signs such as !, /, // and others, but for the sake of clarity these signs have been omitted except for the !, which denotes a *pop* made by pulling the tongue off the hard palate. Also, the / is part of the name of the Ju/Wasi People and is very much like the sound used to make a horse switch from a walk to a canter.

I understand that an orthography of the Ju/Wasi language will be ready in 1990, but even this can only be a collection of words *as they sound* to the orthographer. For example, I found all of the following spellings of the "capital" of Bushmanland in very solid and formal research: Tsumkwe, Tjum!kwe, Sumkwi, Sunki, Chumqui, Tchumkwi, Tshumkwe and Tsumkeve. Three of these spellings were from the same enthnologist!

Further, as to the name of the southern !Kung people, I found Ju/Wasi, Ju/wasi, Ju/Wāsi, Ju/'hoan, Ju/hoan, Ju/Hoan, Dhuwazi, Zhu twa si, Zjuch'hoansi and Zjuc'hoansi.

For the purpose of this book, I have used the simplest words that sound closest to the real ones, and have omitted the variety of "clicks" found.

ACKNOWLEDGMENTS

The author would like to express his usual deep thanks and appreciation to his wife, Fiona Claire Capstick, for her help during the Bushmanland trip and her tireless editing and suggestions as to the manuscript.

Thanks of the warmest kind are due to Dr. Philip Kahl for his patience and fine work in capturing on film some of the days we will see no more.

Dr. Anthony Hall-Martin, Director of Special Services of the South African National Parks Board and a prominent author and conservationist, deserves special thanks for his time and for his wisdom. Thanks, old friend.

Volker and Anke Grellmann, thanks for all your trouble, expense and expertise. It wouldn't have been an elephant book and video without you. We all appreciate your hospitality so much!

Thanks of the highest order are also owed to Roger Olkowski, who kept trying with that Betacam until it was right. Also, the greatest appreciation to Doug and Angi Stephensen, who, between them, kept both our bellies and our horizons full!

I would also like to thank sincerely the staff at Anvo Safaris, Johnny, Jonas, Mateus and the rest of the men and women who made our stay in Bushmanlan so wonderful.

Special thanks to Jerry and Bam Heiner, who were always charming and entertaining, as well as generous in letting us film their hunt. Thanks especially to Bam, who remembered that I love Triscuits and brought a supply some twelve thousand miles!

Ken Wilson, producer and editor of *Capstick—Hunting the African Elephant,* gets special mention for his patience and skill.

It would not have made a book or video without the many

Ju/Wasi Bushmen who helped us and who were so loyal. I wish you better times, my friends.

The most appreciative thanks also go to Arnold Huber, who worked constantly for us to get the Bushmen exposure that we wanted. His work is very much appreciated by all of us.

I would like especially to thank my agent, Richard Curtis of New York City, for his patience and hard work in getting this project off the ground. The same appreciation goes to my editor, Michael Sagalyn of St. Martin's Press, Inc., also of New York, as well as his assistant, Ed Stackler, who took so much of the heavy labor of this book in his stride.

Thank you, all of you.

SANDS *of* SILENCE

CHAPTER

ONE

Namibian sunset.

The dead dog hung transfixed by a moonbeam. Below it, the knuckles of an elephant loomed in the same yellow light as a full moon eased to its zenith, bathing the scene in golden rays almost as bright as daylight. I tapped Volker lightly for the owl-eye, and pointed it over the top of the black .375 Magnum rifle. It rasped slightly against the dry salt on my cheeks as I focused the device and looked through the lenses. Edged in green, the light it drew was astonishing, each blade of the Kalahari-withered grass as sharp as a sword and each jagged stick of bush plated with the same winter-weary edging. In a silent click, I turned off the battery element and quietly handed it back to Volker. He took it with exaggerated slowness and carefully placed it on his lap without turning his head in the least.

Far, far away, I could hear a bushbaby crying on the hot, dry night air, and once there was the closer yap of a black-backed jackal, slicing the cooler wind like a serrated bread knife. From almost a mile away came a quiet cough from the Bushman encampment at Naneh, where perhaps fifty souls lay sleeping by the fires in a swelter of sweat and heat. Certainly they were no hotter than we were, I thought as I eased my bum slightly on the canvas seat of a camp chair inside the blind and collected a black glance from Volker. Above, a satellite drifted as silently as the stars across the gem-filled sky, coming from our left and dying out of sight to our right. I wondered whose it was. Could it *really* see a golf ball at two hundred miles? Who would want to see a golf ball so far away, anyway? My brain scrambled and I furtively fished out my watch from the little pocket I had always questioned the use of. Ten past one. Good. Another fifty minutes before it was my turn to stare at that fool tree that might sprout a monster dog-and-cow-killing leopard. I closed my eyes after a glance at Volker, who was hunkered like a huge heap on the edge of his chair, and was figuring out how to spend all that money from the Pulitzer Prize when I felt it. . . .

It spoke for itself, a thick, strong grip that actually hurt my upper arm. I knew better than to react, just sliding my eyes open an almond sliver and staring straight ahead. I started to shift forward, but the grip increased along with several damned painful tightenings from the huge hand that had grabbed me. Slowly I went over our signals. One nudge or grip meant that the watcher had seen the leopard on the ground, but there was no change in the sere, sandy northern Kalahari that separated us from the tree. Two squeezes or pulses mean that the leopard was in the tree. No, again. But what in hell did a very solid and sustained grip mean? Oh, my! Maybe snake?

We had seen several mambas and caught two puff adders already, but as far as I could see there were none on the floor of the blind, which vastly decreased my sense of immediate foreboding. But what the hell *was* it? I eased my eyes to Volker's furry face, the moon catching in the silver whiskers of his full beard. He sensed my movement, slight though it was, and tightened with the definite message that I was not to move again. Kee-rist, maybe it *was* a snake!

Oh, unspeakables! What do I do now? I looked again out the small gun port where the custom .375 H&H by Musgrave was supported by twin V-sticks, but saw nothing. The moon streamed down as if it were melting, but I could see nothing. The dog was intact. The elephant meat had not been touched. There was nothing between us and the tree. So *what!* Quietly, I eased my glance toward Volker. He was staring straight out of my porthole of the tent and bush blind. But at what? I looked again. Dammit, when they built this mother they should have left a clear view instead of letting that blob of branches or whatsis partially obscure my seeing hole! Damn! But then it hit me. The blob had not been there before. What the hell was it? Without looking again, I knew. . . .

I sat in frozen shock for perhaps a second, at which point

it was time to consider my options. I could see the home papers now: IDIOT HUNTER KILLED IN LEOPARD BLIND! Or maybe BUNGLING BWANA BASHED? Perhaps an upper-class, more niggardly headline would shout, NITWIT AUTHOR INGESTED. Yet, as I stared at the blob about three feet from my nose, I started to get the idea that perhaps Volker and I could bring a weapon to bear before what was obviously a lioness could tear apart the outer tent and kill us. For once I was beginning to agree with Volker that the idea of using tents as blind foundation wasn't so crazy after all.

She was no more than a yard away, now that I focused on her. Motionless, she stared in as hard as we stared out. As I am sure Grellmann's brain had done, I went over our arsenal mentally. Let's see. . . . There was the .375, but we could never get it off the V-posts in time to get a shot from inside a zipped tent. There was the .470 Nitro Express elephant gun, a side-by-side double out of Famars by Champlin, which was loaded with solid bullets and which would sure do the trick, but it would make too much noise to ease it from its propped-up position in my corner of the canvas. There was always the shotgun, stoked with No. 1 buck, but it was behind me, and the lioness was looking at me from a yard away. Volker had his old .458 Winchester as well as a shotgun, but what he didn't tell me at the time—perhaps he himself had forgotten—was that he had a .44 Magnum revolver that I had never seen, possibly kept in case I didn't pay my bill. I didn't know about the revolver, and all of the other arms were too noisy to move, so I figured we could do little else but look back at what I was sure was an astonished lioness.

On second thought, perhaps she had not been able to make out what we were. I certainly hoped so. She was far too close for comfort. But she was close enough to study. She had a strange head, less linear and more blocky than that of the usual lioness, and she had some odd markings on what I could see of her neck, sort of darker splotches in the moonlight. I wondered if she had brought along the family to the festivities, and hoped that she was a lone Jezebel out for an evening on her own. Actually, measuring the predicament, I figured that we could get one or another of the guns free before she ripped off the tent face. But, then, maybe we couldn't. If she attacked the front of the tent, maybe all the weapons would end up under folds of canvas and we would be left to show and tell.

A brace of eternities drifted by without a move from either party when, in an instant, she doubled like a horizontal, greased Indian Rope Trick and faded away to the rear of the tent/blind. Unfortunately, a soft sound of a heavy body in dry leaves whispered like a cobra, and if you strained, you could hear her harsh breathing on the hot night air. Volker took his hand away, and the blood started to circulate in my arm again.

There were things over the next two hours I did think of, but sleep wasn't one of them. When we were sure—or at least when *I* was sure—that the lioness wouldn't come back, I leaned over to Volker and whispered that there was sure no hope of the village-raiding leopard coming that night, what with that lioness around. He looked at me kind of queerly, but obviously had decided to pack it in anyway. After all, we had been hunting elephant all day in what were at least 115-degree temperatures, and to have lasted until 4:00 A.M. was a pretty good showing. That was twenty-three hours of various hunting, after all.

He picked up his shotgun, and I heard the nasty metal sound as the safety was disengaged under his finger, and he eased out the side of the tent flap. He had a broad look around while I gathered up more weapons than the D-Day invasion toted and squeezed out beside him. He loomed over me like a strange, golden ostrich over a plover. "Now," he said in his kindliest tone, the one he used with imbeciles, "What's this about lionesses?"

"But surely you saw her?" I asked incredulously. "Christ, she was practically a boarder! You mean you didn't see her?"

"I saw the biggest leopard I ever saw in my life, but I didn't see any lionesses. Did you think . . ."

"Naw," I said, mentally scrambling for some arguing space. "I was just asking what you saw. Big one, wasn't she? Uh, I mean *him!*"

"By the spoor alone, he's got to go over eight feet, maybe

closer to nine. *Ach!* The biggest goddam leopard I ever saw. . . ."

He took the checkered black five-cell torch from my hand and swept it around the perimeter of the opening and then to the ground near the front of the blind. For a couple of seconds it stayed on the dead dog and flickered down to the elephant foot. Then he swept the sandy earth with the beam and gave a low whistle.

"Never saw prints like these. He's as big as a lioness, I'll give you that. But look here. No question it was a male leopard." I looked. And blinked. They were leopard pugs, okay. Imagine that the sonofabitch had been too *close* to shoot! "Maybe from my angle I had a better look at him than you did out of your corner," said Volker, striding off in his usual giant-killing steps to the bush track that led back to the car. "But I'll tell you this— he won't be back again. He's had a good whiff of us. No way he'll come back."

It was a long ride home, perhaps an hour, as false dawn gave an odd, ethereal edge to the outlines of the fluttering nightjars, sooty wraiths that flushed from just ahead of the tires. Owls flickered alongside the hunting car, picking up startled mice. We saw the tiny, bloodshot eyes of the main camp at Klein Dobe just as dawn really started trying. Already the camp staff were up in the growing light, starting cooking fires and brewing coffee for them that takes it. Personally, an icy beer would have fulfilled my wildest dreams. And so it did.

I creaked from the freezer—which doesn't *really* freeze anything in the Eastern Bushmanland heat—to our tent, where I gave a rousing Fiona a somewhat-less-than-Hollywood kiss. "Did you get him?" she asked. A single look told her that her boy needed a little bit of head-patting.

"Not exactly," I said mysteriously. "I could have taken one hell of a lioness, but she was too close." When the shower water had turned from roan to semi-clear and I had blown the roosting detritus out of my mustache, I wandered down to a nauseatingly jolly breakfast. Even Volker was there, placing a flanking movement on enough eggs and sausage to keep a Bushman clan solvent. Guinea fowl were churring down by the water point, and a lovesick shrike was competing with the weaver birds for notice in an unnoticing world. I felt like something you kick sand over and quietly walk away from.

"Let's saddle up," said Phil, obstreperous as ever. "Want to catch these few minutes of proper light."

"Yeah," agreed Robert Olkowski. "Let's push off."

"Look, why don't you guys go to the game reserve or some-place today? I don't feel photogenic. Run along and play with your lenses, humm?" An egg I had chosen from the fried pile was looking at me quite unkindly.

"Hey," said Phil, bright-eyed from a decent night's sleep without my snoring to keep the lions away, "I thought we were here to take pictures of you, Bwana."

"Yeah," Roger chimed in. "Do you wanna make this video or not?"

I considered the blissful alternative, then thought of Ken Wilson and all his hungry brood. "You mean you want to keep after that elephant we tracked yesterday? Talk some sense into these neophytes, Volker." I put the egg's eye out with a single

Dr. M. Philip Kahl, the still photographer, in Bushman garb.

Roger Olkowski.

slash of my fork. It flowed down the white perimeter, orange and injured.

"Not for me to decide if you shirk your duty or not," said Volker helpfully. "If you don't want to go out, despite the bucks you are paying, I would be happier in my bed." Nice guy, Volker. What I need is another Volker.

"Of course," he said around several bushels of bacon, "maybe this is a hundred-pounder. Who knows until we have caught up with him?"

Well, that settled it. I strapped on the ammo belt, snugged down my hat, and went for my rifles. I beat everybody to the hunting vehicle, but it was not discovered until I was a couple of miles out of camp that I was still barefoot.

It was a great year for safari, 1989, considering that I was not a professional hunter anymore. In June, I had gone with old pal Mick Arsenault of Dallas—at the time—and frozen my nevermind off for two weeks in a steel rondaval on a Namibian ranch while Mick collected two excellent gemsbuck, the giant southern oryx, as well as taking a left and a right on bull kudu. Now, what do you say to a guy who has doubled on two excellent kudu? Right. Nothing. Not hunting big game, I was loath to climb the junior Himalayas on the Gobabis ranch, but had a wonderful time with a tame Bushman named Fritz hunting dassies, rock rabbits, or hyrax, whatever you want to call the woodchuck-sized critters that seethe through the most inhospitable cliffs of south-central Namibia.

I also had some of the finest birdshooting of my life in company with Mick and Gary Haselau, another old friend, shooting (at) the very fast and very thirsty Namaqua sand grouse that are in the millions in the area. I developed a recoil scar on my right shoulder that will follow me to the crematorium, and I will show it to anyone who asks how the birdshooting is in Namibia. We shot at a couple of the few water holes where the sand grouse drink, and there were so many birds that we didn't beat them up very badly at all. Of course, there are bag limits, but they are generous. After a while, we only shot at birds that would fall into a specific circle of twenty-five yards, if that gives you some idea of the shooting quality.

After my trip with Mick—garnished with the beauty of Cape Town and its seafood—I had a twenty-one-day trip called the Dunn's Celebrity Safari, which took place in Botswana with Gordon Cundill's firm, Hunters Africa. The idea was that I would host the clients from their arrival in Johannesburg until their departure, which worked out very well.

Among the hunters were Dr. Bruce Melrose, who mostly hunted with my old buddy George Hoffman, John and Mary Dicken of Tennessee, who have become old pals, and Frank Stallone, brother of Sylvester. John Northcote, who arguably holds the greatest tenure of all practicing professional hunters in Africa, hunted John and Mary Dicken to a terrific collection of trophies, whereas Gordon Cundill Hisself floated through the safari going out, as I did, with Frank Stallone, Bruce Melrose, and the Dickens. Actually, it was a bang-up trip, and everybody took lion—or could have—Frank Stallone deciding that he really shouldn't kill his birth sign despite long tracking of three superb, platinum-maned males, which were finally caught up with. Peter Hepburn, one of the best professional hunters I have ever seen, took Frank under his wing with Tony Colagreco, a Californian restaurant entrepreneur who was along to observe.

The problem was that the Celebrity Safari finished up on September 23, and I was to go to Windhoek and Bushmanland in the very early hours of the twenty-fifth of the same month. Yet, thanks to Fifi, all clients—now friends—were properly accommodated in the Sandton Sun Hotel and seen off. Incidentally, if you ever come to South Africa, I recommend you choose a "fringe" hotel, as the downtown area of Johannesburg has become positively dangerous with street crime.

Dr. Phil Kahl had arrived, or pitched up as we would say in Africa, on the twenty-third to get his skull screwed down again from jet lag, and we picked him up at Jan Smuts, the international airport. Of course, he had "Baby," the 600-mm lens with which he does a great deal of his work, cradled in loving arms. As far as I know, he slept with it, although it is anybody's guess whether it joined him in the shower. Phil immediately went to bed despite the washing-machine noises as Fifi redid my bush clothes, which were still desiring something, if only in her gaze.

I was pleasantly tired, pleased that things had gone well. Anytime one makes lasting friends, it has been a good trip. I thought back on some of the episodes that were less than those I would have chosen, like the morning that Bruce, George, Gordon, and I went lion hunting. . . .

Gordon and I had found a very fine bull kudu pulled down by what seemed a lone lioness. It was within fifty yards of the Chobe River, and the bush was very thick. Gordon and I went in with rifles bared. After fifty yards, according to the perched vultures, the lioness was still on the kill, but we couldn't see whether or not she had whistled up her old man for a bit of fresh victuals. On our way to the kill, we both noticed a sort of hollow windfall, almost like a Bushman shelter that had been abandoned, although it was a natural formation. What a superior place to leave lion cubs while the old lady fed, we both thought, and signaled by a lifting of sweat-caked eyebrows. As we approached the kill, vultures flapped off and we heard a very definite rumble of lioness. She was rather old, beyond having young, but only when confronted by us did she ease off into the riverine bush.

The next morning, when it was still as cold as a skinned pole, we were at the edge of the cover, about ten miles from camp on the Chobe River. Bruce Melrose had killed a zebra the day before, some two miles from the natural kill, and possibly there would be something chewing on the carcass. Through very hazy logic, which determined that meat used for bait might, in other circumstances, be consumed by the local indigenous human population, baiting is illegal in Botswana. This stupid law matches the statute in which the *madallas* or tribal elders decided that the safari season should end September 18 or 19, thus losing untold thousands if not millions of U.S. dollars on the simplistic principle that this is the time when most plains game, such as antelopes, drop their young.

Of course, being horn and not meat oriented, safari hunters did not covet either young or females as did the tribal elders themselves, who had no interest in trophies or horns, the ladies and children are fair game as opposed to *regulated* sport hunting for males. The season was closed during a most productive time, the visibility being better and the revenues produced more lucrative for the people in terms of hunting licenses and trophy fees.

Rural bush Africans are interested in *nyama*. Meat. Flesh. Age or sex of the animal doesn't matter. Thus they cheat the paying safari hunter as well as themselves. But this is Africa. In emerging—or, as is the financial case in many newly independent lands, submerging—countries, logic has little to do with game laws. Perhaps this is why it is still Africa, with all of its seemingly insurmountable problems.

These problems will continue as long as such illogical thinking persists. This is forever, if you ask me.

There was nothing on Bruce's zebra, so there was all the more reason that there should be lions on the dead bull kudu that the lioness had killed. Walking back to the track, we had given the dead kudu an hour to settle down with what we hoped was a collection of lions, because the wind was now in our favor, whereas we had whisked through at dawn as it was blowing behind us.

We covered almost a mile before Gordon Cundill turned the hunting car off the dirt track and we began to walk the remaining mile to the kudu.

We took our time, Gordon going first, then George Hoffman and Bruce Melrose. Gordon had his .500 Nitro, and of course George had his namesake, the .416 Hoffman. Bruce held some sort of exotic Weatherby that we teased him about, but there was no question that he killed what he shot at. I think his was the .378 which would reduce me into recoiled pulp, and Bruce was smaller than I was.

Slowly we proceeded, parting branches that Gordon had parted and George had parted and Bruce had parted. It was the essence of hunting, each branch bringing us closer to where at least we knew there were lions, big African cats that could kill you and make all your honorary degrees posthumous. It was hunting at its best; dangerous and unknown.

Off to the right was a hollow little bower that Gordon and I had seen the day before. Gordon had already passed it by a few feet, and George was right in front of the entrance, with Bruce a couple of feet away.

It happened in a heartbeat. George immediately covered the front of the tangle a couple of feet away. I could hear his fervent "Jesus! Lion!" which isn't a prayer even to a born-again Christian like George, but it sure told us plenty. Instantly—and I do not misuse the term—the bower was covered by an initial strike capability of at least 22,000 pounds of bullet muzzle energy from four major firearms.

Thanks to Almighty that momma was eating kudu fillets and not home, or somebody would have gotten it. From a couple of feet, there is almost no way to lull an animal the size of a lioness to death with even multiple shots unless they hit the brain, a cavity even smaller than our own for having been there in the first place. Hydrostatic shock, even from some of the most highly touted rifles, does not work. Believe my scars. . . .

Inside the branch shelter were four lion cubs, unharmed, as large a dose of bad news as you are likely to get no matter where you hunt in Africa. Female lions are not casual with their cubs, believe me. Momma was nearby, and the smallest whimper of the smallest of the cubs would mean a real, no-kidding, very un-Elsa charge, and somebody might get terminally hurt and a lady lion would get killed, if we were lucky.

When I say that we backed off from that swirl of deeply shaded branches, I do not put you on. A mouse never backtracked from a big tomcat as silently. I noticed that nobody put the safety of his rifle back on.

At fifteen yards, Gordon grabbed Bruce Melrose by the collar and brought him up to the kudu kill, about twenty yards away. There were very un-kudu-like patches of, well, lion-colored hide, and the wind held. But there was no male. Perhaps he had found the favors of another female—there were two eating their bellies full—but he was not there. Becoming aware of us, the two females ran a couple of yards from the kill and stopped, facing us. We backed off, believe me. We backed off like nobody has ever backed off. When it comes to off-backing I hold the Olympic record, closely followed by Cundill, Hoffman, and Melrose. But I broke the tape first.

Bruce later killed a honey of a lion after losing a shot at one that was somewhat aquatic. Yet I suppose there is another place to tell these tales, as well as that of John Dicken, who killed his lion when out after the aquatic antelope, the sitatunga, a white one, if you can believe it—the sitatunga, not the lion.

I really only had a day before I left the Celebrity Hunt and headed for South-West Africa, as it was then called, with Phil. I took three each of bush shirts and shorts as well as a couple of long pants for the aircraft, the usual tendency being to over-pack. I also had the usual amaze-the-natives stuff such as the cold-light wands (which amaze me, never mind the natives, I love 'em), as well as my new Capstick African Damascus knife by Rob Charlton of Damascus USA, who supplies raw Damascus billets to the trade as well as making his own fine knives.

I have always secretly hated the late Robert Ruark because he had a Spanish castle from which to plan his Rover Boys forays, and I just had to make do from a town house. Spanish castle be damned, Phil and I took off on the twenty-fifth of September, 1989, from Jan Smuts Airport after having gotten up at something like four before the cock crows. I call it the painful time. Phil was unable to speak until we were halfway to the airport.

Of course, I had to get export permits for my firearms, and this is as good a time as any to tell you about the tools of my trade. . . .

My .470 Nitro Express double was stolen on Thanksgiving 1974 from my Florida town house, a fine rifle that I had used on, shall we say, imminent occasions. I had always wanted to replace it, but I might as well have wished for the holy grail until *Death in the Long Grass* came out. That book improved my financial outlook as it still, quite amazingly, does. The original rifle was an Evans, not a frou-frou collection of engraving but a working gun, of which it did plenty. I had used a .470 Nitro in cropping elephants, as well as the .500 Nitro 3", but I found the .470 the best of all worlds.

I was at the Safari Club International Show at Las Vegas, personalizing leatherbound books, when I bumped into George Caswell of Champlin Arms. Sure, and bumping into George Caswell is like an alcoholic bumping into a whiskey wagon. He usually has enough double rifles of fine quality to sell by the pound, but I had had a good year and liked a particular double he had on show.

It was the prototype of the Champlin-Famars deal between George and the Famars people of Italy, in my beloved .470 Nitro caliber, and it was ever so slightly shopworn. Slightly used but not abused, as the used-car people would call it. Well, I bought it. It was twelve grand, but it was a hell of a rifle, shooting iron-sighted sixty-meter groups of a touch over an inch. In fact, number 763, produced by Abbiatico and Salvinelli (Famars) is as fine a double as I shall find on an Anson and Deely action box lock,

Champlin-Famars .470 Nitro Express double rifle.

which is what Rigby used all those many years ago in their bloom. It is proper weight, at about eleven pounds, has a choice of ivory or plain bead, and handles like a newborn babe when it is asleep.

I must inject that we are in fact speaking of an elephant gun. The first chance I had to fire it was with no benchrest available, so I improvised a rest out of a TV table, towels, and a motor-scooter tire. The first three groups prompted me to enshrine the target in a safe on letterhead paper, which, in fact, I did. But then I made a mistake. . . .

I had fired three rounds through each barrel, right and left, and I did the unspeakable, the unthinkable. I doubled it. Whether or not it was my fault by hitting both triggers at once or whether it was jarred off by recoil, to this day I don't know. Yet I can assure you that both went off at once. Maybe there is a rib cage that can withstand 150 grains of cordite, I don't know, but for sure it isn't mine.

Just like a kid who bellyflops or is kicked from a horse, I went back to the bench. I shot eighteen more rounds of Kynoch, although it hurt, to say the least. I shouldn't have done that. . . .

A few days went by, and the pain got worse. After a week I couldn't breathe properly and, in imagined extremis, asked Fifi to take me to the doctor. Somehow I managed the three stories up to his offices as the elevator was inoperable. A chest X ray showed as nice a broken rib as you could hope for, sort of a greenstick break that had somehow broken outward instead of penetrating my lung. A handful of Voltaren made me more comfortable if not wiser.

There was another new gun, which I never had a chance to use on the trip, although I carried it along at all times except when actually spooring elephant. Some months before the trip, through the courtesy of Lt. Gen. Denis Earp, I had a chance to visit the gunmaking plant of Musgrave, which was some hours south of my Pretoria home. We were greeted by Abe Koch, the general manager, who so impressed me with their general and custom shops that I ordered a .375 H&H Magnum on a Mauser action.

Now, really, when it was finished, I have never seen a pret-

The author firing the custom Musgrave .375 H&H with octagonal barrel.

tier or more functional rifle. I have owned custom guns before, but nobody ever put one together like Musgrave did. Owing to the UN sanctions against armaments, Musgrave has had its problems in exporting its wares, but this seems as if it won't go on very long, since, as of this writing, President F. W. de Klerk has just returned from Washington. Musgrave used Grade V Turkish walnut and inscribed on it my personal serial number, PHC-1, as well as inlaying my name in gold on the top of the octagonal barrel. I was quite puritan about the engraving, although Musgrave has some of the best chisel-men in the world. Just the front of the chamber, the magazine floor plate and the bolt knurl were done, but oh, so tastefully, in a soft scroll. Of course, engraving doesn't add anything to the shooting characteristics of a rifle, but coupled with a Timney adjustable trigger and the rigidity of an octagonal barrel, PHC-1 will shoot one-inch groups at one hundred meters with factory ammo all day long. Believe me, when sanctions go, and they will, possibly by the publication date of this book, the best deal in the world is with Musgrave of Bloemfontein, South Africa. The rand-dollar exchange assures that.

I cropped some thirty zebra with this rifle in Botswana in '89, and with A-Square ammunition in the .375 H&H I never had a lost animal. Those of you with some safari experience realize what this means: the zebra is possibly, pound-for-pound, the hardest animal to bring down with one shot in Africa.

Phil and I left South Africa on the twenty-fifth and arrived at Windhoek, the capital of what was then South-West Africa, at about eleven o'clock, where Volker met us. Upon departure from South Africa, Phil did his usual take-my-children-take-my-wife-but-don't-touch-the-film bit. Finally he got his several hundred rolls hand-examined, but it was hair, teeth and eyes all the way. According to Phil, never let *any* of your film be exposed to the X-ray machines at airports, particularly if you have several international layovers. If you are a professional, be prepared to die for it. Sure as hell it will be fogged, maybe not noticeably from the first machine, but from an accumulation of X rays. Phil once went through a blank refusal in, I think, Zimbabwe. He declared that he would take the bus home, which I am sure he would have done, but finally the security people let up, and Phil made his plane.

We had some coffee and a cold one at Volker's home, a lovely place in Windhoek where Anke had laid out refreshments of sandwiches and biltong, the shade-dried meat of southern Africa. On the way back to the airport we talked politics, something I would as soon leave alone. Yet this was part of our visit. It, of course, centered on the election that was supposed to take place chiefly beween the South West Africa People's Organization (SWAPO), which was Marxist, and rather a conglomerate of parties under the acronym of DTA, which is the Democratic Turnhalle Alliance, a moderate group, among many other independent parties. At the time, the country was occupied by UNTAG, the United Nations Transition Assistance Group, composed of "unbiased" UN people from such places as Finland and Kenya, who hate the South Africans, who had previous mandate over the country after Germany lost it at the end of World War I. Of course, many of these volunteer troops joined the UN forces because by doing so they were able to buy an expensive automobile and then import it to their home countries tax-free. Their legacy was AIDS, which they have taken home with them, as well as unnumbered illegitimate children whom they left behind. Maybe it's worth AIDS to bring home a tax-free Maserati. . . .

As you will gather, I have little personal time for the machinations of the UN. Perhaps the greatest laugh came when Australian troops made a combat landing on Windhoek Airport and then fanned out to "secure their perimeter." Typical of the UN, somebody hadn't gotten the word. A combat landing on Windhoek is about the same as doing so at Newark Airport. Still, they took their imported cars home.

Enough of politics.

Phil and I came in on SAA flight 701, having left home at 3:35 A.M., and were at Jan Smuts Airport at 5:45 for a 6:30 departure, leaving enough time for the guns and cameras to be properly inspected. Of course, somebody in the passport section had overslept, and it was not until five of six that it was opened.

After leaving Anke and Volker at the airport, we took a charter plane piloted by Maurice van Zyl and finally arrived at Tsumkwe, the so-called capital of Bushmanland, an hour and a half later and three hundred kilometers away from Windhoek. Our plane was a Cessna 310, which took all of our hand luggage including Phil's cameras, not an easy feat. Of course, when we arrived we didn't know who was whom—let alone where we were—and I almost hugged a departing schoolteacher under the impression that she was Angi Stephensen, sent from camp to collect us.

Angi pitched up a couple of minutes later in a bronchial Land-Rover that dislayed all symptoms of extremis. The strip at Tsumkwe was rather short on first-class lounges—in fact, in lounges at all. So we piled in the terminal Land-Rover and had got about two hundred yards when it quit.

I have always subscribed to the thought that one should never try to repair a friend's car, on the theory that there is no way to win. If you fix it, the owner will say that the problem was the next thing he or she was going to check. If you fail, it is your fault alone since it could have been fixed if only one had left the goddam thing alone.

The sand was deep. Phil and I were thirsty. Bushman women stood by. Perhaps sharpening their knives. It was getting hotter and I was getting thirstier. So was Phil. If you want to get a Land-Rover fixed, I do not recommend Tsumkwe. It does have a gas station that fills the large, four-wheel-drive Kenyan vehicles, but I suspect they have never lifted a hood—excuse me, *bonnet*.

Angi, a trim and attractive German blonde, was clearly at her wits' end. By this time I had had a chance to figure out what it might be, and, supposing that we might spend a couple of weeks here, I broke my own rule.

"How many petrol tanks does this car have?" I asked.

"I don't know," said Angi.

"Well, let's take this little lever and twitch it over here." The engine boiled to life. I was at least today's hero. Nobody

Without a Toyota Land Cruiser it would be impossible to hunt elephant in Namibia because of the distances involved.

had mentioned that I had been a professional hunter and should know what was wrong in the first place. I always maintained that I was a lucky hunter, not a skilled one as far as mechanics were involved.

After what seemed perhaps a thousand miles, we passed Klein Dobe pan on our left and Angi reckoned that it was only a few kilometers to camp. At last it showed up, flying a most irregular flag, one that I had seen before, but couldn't place in my repertoire of star and stripes and banners. It turned out to be the Tennessee state flag, which meant that Hanley Sayers was in camp and holding court.

The first people to greet us in the twilight were Bam and Jerry Heiner. It somehow seemed odd as hell to have them out here in nowhere when where I had last seen them was Reno, Nevada. Bam was her usual pretty, vivacious self, and Jerry not a whit less charming than normal. "You wanna watch the amputation?" Jerry asked me after our usual hugs and such.

"No, Hanley Sayers is operating on Glen, who screwed up

Camp, as first seen, with Tennessee flag signifying Hanley Sayers was there.

Bam and Jerry Heiner.

his thumb while sharpening a knife. Got a sharp thumb for his trouble."

I wondered, outside the grass thatch encampment, whether an amputation or a cold beer was precedential. I decided on the cold beer first, as did Phil, and then proceeded to the festivities.

There was little time to introduce ourselves as Hanley already had Glen's thumb across his knee. Of course, amputation had been an overstatement, but from the look of Glen's opposable digit, there was every reason for the stitches that Hanley was about to render. I introduced myself and offered to help.

"Grab his arm above the wrist," said Hanley. "This probably won't feel too good."

I did as instructed, but it was not necessary. I wondered about infection and released the video man's arm and hied off to the bar for some vodka, which I trickled over the gore-oozing wound flap.

Hanley finished his first stitch of five, and tied it off like a pro. I was impressed, knowing as I did all there was to know about stitches in safari camps. Glen never made a sound.

After the mechanics were finished, several volunteers made better use of the vodka. Phil and I retired for the moment in the half-light and dragged our stuff over to the tent that Volker usually occupied, a standard client's tent, with extra space, in green canvas with a fly sheet. Off the rear was an *en suite* bathroom and shower. It would do just fine.

Of course, the camp was crowded beyond its usual capacity. Jerry and Bam had agreed that we might come early and, in fact, send Roger Olkowski ahead, which made three in excess, then there were Phil and me, as well as Hanley and Glen and Doug and Angi. This certainly was not the normal state of affairs, given that the camp would usually cater to, at most, a hunter and his wife.

Klein Dobe camp.

The tentage at Klein Dobe was excellent and spacious with an *en suite* bathroom and shower.

Phil had one of his security crises (other than removing "Baby" from his lap), his first of the trip. What should he do with three hundred rands of South African currency? Also, he had translated all his credit card numbers into a code that he had lost. All that remained was his telephone credit card. After commenting that his luggage had pulled a knife, Phil also dissolved in laughter and suggested that the only thing to do was call the operator. Of course there were as many phones as operators in Bushmanland: none.

We had a super dinner of oxtail broiled with gravy, and got to know Hanley, Glen, Roger, Doug and Angi. Replete, we went to an early bed, disturbing only Phil, who thought that my snoring was the equal of, and perhaps superior to, any he had ever heard.

The next morning dawned with what would prove to be the usual heat; it was too hot to lie in bed after five-thirty. The guinea fowl were watering with their usual ground-marbles-and-

Author with the Heiners.

Model-A-starter sound. The Christmas beetles had already started with their cicada whine as the monstrous red sun ratcheted its way over the shaggy horizon, bigger than other suns and twice as bloody.

I had the look around that twilight had denied us yesterday evening. The grass around the camp was as dead as charity, and the horizons edged with sere, dry, thirsty bush. There were three client's tents, beautiful in their early-morning verdance of green canvas tinged with orange light, then the spacious and airy dining hut, built of thatch and mopane-wood poles. Nearby sat the kitchen with its marvels, and another hut, which nobody had

26

ever found of any use since the icy winds of winter had snatched and bitten with long, white teeth at fatigued elephant hunters trying to have some dinner in the freezing earlier months.

All about was sand, and not mere sand, but some of the oldest sand on earth. This was eastern Bushmanland only now. For billions of years it had been what was called by geologists Gondwanaland, the Mother of All Continents. It was from here, the epicenter, that the continents had broken loose on their journey of continental drift. They all fitted in here, South America, Europe and the rest. The sand was so old that I knew it wouldn't do for cement; it was too rounded through the action of unthought-of eons. Somehow, it was dirty, yet clean, a squeaking stuff that found every line of the face, every pore of the shoe, as smooth as obsidian and as hot as fresh lava.

What more likely place to find the most ancient people than in the most ancient place? This was the home of the Bushmen, or at least of the last of them to yield to the insane pressures of the outside world.

Phil and I arrived at dinner after a day of sorting out cameras, film, rifles, ammo and the usual crap that comes on safari with me and that will never be used, except just that once. Thus I had brought it, overpacking as usual. I had had a chance to speak with Jerry and Bam and found to my disappointment that Jerry had already taken his elephant, which Roger had videoed, but not to his satisfaction. "Christ," he said in obvious irritation, "I was the odd man out! The professional hunter had nothing on his mind but killing an elephant, no matter where the camera was. You know, Peter, it's not like we shoot an elephant every day!" I listened to what had happened. Actually, it wasn't that bad a piece of video when I saw it. Jerry's elephant could have been better placed, but after all, it was elephant hunting. And it was Roger's first trip.

Jerry had been professionally hunted by a young man, Gerhard Liedtke, a German national. Gerhard was a very nice guy, but very ill at ease with the English language. He had previously hunted German clients, but this was, as far as I could determine, his first English-speaker. Having played host to Italian clients more times than I could remember, I recalled being given those safaris because I spoke fluent Spanish. Of course, the safari company owners figured, if he speaks Spanish he will have no trouble with Italian, since they're both Romance languages. Actually, it worked out fairly well, though I'm sure I have no idea why.

Over dinner and a couple of cool ones after, I was able to figure out what Roger's problems were. First off, he had lacked equipment, the "shoe" to his tripod being missing. This I was able to remedy for about two weeks with a Lufthansa baggage strap that affixed his camera to the tripod solidly. Second, we determined that in making a video, we would have to work around Roger and Phil, rather than have them work around us. The most important thing was how the video and the stills turned out, but I soon discovered that we had something of a conflict of interest because Phil wanted the same prime shots that Roger did, but Phil's cameras made some noise that would be picked up on the video. We were never able to solve this in the field, but Ken Wilson was able to come to grips with the dilemma in Hollywood, where he edited out all of the mechanical whirring of Phil's motor drive.

For five days or so, Roger's Betacam had broken down due to the lack of a modification that had become necessary on his model. It was set right in Windhoek at the price of two charters, one flight in either direction, which wasn't a small expenditure. The experts in Windhoek, knowing the speed necessary, had made the change with a strip of Coca-Cola tin, and it worked perfectly. For a while . . .

Later that evening we tried to work out schedules of who would be with whom and when, coming up with a fairly precise timetable. I wanted to get the most possible footage of the Bushmen making snares and poisoning arrows, or whatever Bushmen do in their spare time, and I had high hopes of being able to videotape Jerry Heiner taking a leopard, if he were so lucky. Working with Arnie, we laid on a couple of Bushmen for the poisoned-arrow sequence for the morning, after we got back from checking the leopard bait that Gerhard had already hung for Jerry. Hanley had left before dawn that morning, back at fly camp to try to get a good elephant, as most activity seemed to be some four hours south of camp, past the Nai-Nai Pan and in a flowage of seasonal water that was green with elephant fodder.

Volker was still back in Windhoek since I couldn't hunt until the other clients were finished with their safaris, which was okay with me, because it gave all that much more opportunity to the video man. Finally, with everything in a pretty good state of preparedness, Phil and I sacked in at about ten that evening. Tomorrow we would start the great adventure.

CHAPTER

Map of Bushmanland with poisoned arrows, ivory-handled Charlton Damascus knife, .470 Nitro cartridge, and a recovered bullet.

Namibia is one of the most underpopulated countries of the world, with a human density about that of Outer Mongolia. Of course, its very nature makes Namibia sparse; it has the Namib Desert to the west and the northern Kalahari of Botswana to the east, where it forms a border composed of merely a fence that Bushmen may pass without passports as they will.

Probably the best way to find Namibia on a map is to go to the top left of the Republic of South Africa and look for one hell of a big blob. It is bordered on the north by Angola, where some thirty thousand people have been killed in both a civil war and a war of incursion since 1966. We have said that in the east it is bordered mostly by Botswana, formerly the Bechuanaland Protectorate of Great Britain, and in the south by South Africa. Namibia, at the time of this safari, was under South African administration and was called South-West Africa rather than Namibia, which is a UN name taken from the Nama language meaning Place of Thirst, roughly, referring to the desert. Also, Namibia has a very international northeast finger called the Caprivi Strip, after Count Caprivi, a luminary of his time. Because there is only one port in the entire country, Walvis Bay, Germany asked for and got a thoroughfare to the Zambezi and the Atlantic via the Caprivi Strip, which comes to a common border with Botswana and Zimbabwe, the latter of which was the old Southern Rhodesia, then Rhodesia. I hope this is confusing enough.

The total area of Namibia is about 318,261 square miles, which makes it considerably bigger than your backyard. This is almost four times the size of the United Kingdom, which itself is rather larger than a breadbox.

The reason that Namibia is so lightly populated is that only about 32 percent of the country has more than four 100-millimeter cigarette packs of rain per annum.

Whites are the second largest group of the population of Namibia, at about 100,000, outnumbered by the Ovambos some four times. There are Damaras, Hereros, Kavangos, Namas, mixed-blood coloreds, East Caprivians, Bushmen, Rehoboth Basters (who are of mixed Hottentot blood, and their name does not imply illegitimacy), as well as Kaokolanders, Tswanas and others.

Namibia has tremendous diamond deposits, and many stones are picked up on the beach near the Orange River border with South Africa. It also has gold, uranium, tin, lead, copper and a whole host of minerals. It has a lot of cattle and karakul sheep also. But this isn't a guidebook. . . .

Among the dates every young girl should know are the following: In 1486 the place was discovered by Diogo Cão, a Portuguese navigator. At Cape Cross on the Atlantic coast, he erected a limestone cross that became badly weathered and was eventually replaced by the Germans with a granite one. In 1487, Bartholomeu Dias stopped at several points on the coast. In 1842, German missionaries arrived and taught otherwise happy people that they should wear pants and shirts, leaving behind the usual mayhem that missionaries leave in trying to impart Christianity to otherwise untainted folk.

The Germans, under their colonial scheme, which was not very different from Britain's, arrived in strength in 1884–85 and occupied the territory known for decades as German Southwest Africa. That in 1904 the Hereros revolted against German colonial rule, leaving more than 80,000 dead Hereros through no-quarter massacre, would seem that the Germans were a bit harsh as rulers. Eighty thousand are a lot of corpses. . . .

In 1919, under the Treaty of Versailles, Germany lost her territories and colonies, and the next year South-West Africa was placed under South African administration as a "Class C" mandated territory by the League of Nations, which, incidentally, suggested the same rules of separate development that the much-hated *"apartheid"* of the Republic of South Africa adopted. Interesting.

The guerrilla war that claimed so many lives began in 1966 and was to last for twenty-three years, during which there was heavy involvement of Angola-based "freedom fighters" who tried to make the country ungovernable, and who were backed by the Soviet Union using Cubans and other communist/socialist forces as surrogates. There was complete involvement of the capitalist South African Defence Force as opposition.

It was not until 1989 that UN Resolution 435 was implemented for independence, in November of 1989, about a week after we cleared out.

Currently there are about fifty political parties in Namibia. But the main ones are the Marxist SWAPO and the more liberal DTA.

The first Bushman I saw was stone drunk. He was lying on the side of the road some five hundred yards from camp at Klein Dobe. A hundred yards ahead was a small encampment of his people, chipping ostrich-shell beads and grinding holes through them, as well as tanning leather. What the leather would be for besides curios I didn't know; certainly all the encampment wore cast-off European clothes and T-shirts that proclaimed the excellence of various political parties, not that the Bushmen would have had a clue as they almost to a man couldn't read.

There were mothers breast-feeding their children by flipping a flat dug over their shoulders, and old people motionless in the morning sun, somehow less than I expected from Volker's small and golden people. There were even dogs, asleep in the cool sunshine, waiting for somebody to drop something. As I watched, an old woman lit a cylinder made from a section of chromed bicycle handle stuffed with tobacco and took ferocious draughts of the raw, dark, natural weed. She coughed and almost fell over. So these were the !Kung Bushmen.

Phil took some close-ups of the people making the ostrich

shell beads, as well as some shots of general camp life, and I could tell that he was quietly disappointed too. Roger didn't even unlimber the Betacam; he had been here for a week.

I was no stranger to Bushmen. For two years, eighteen and nineteen years before this trip, I employed several of them in the southern and central Kalahari as trackers when I was a professional hunter in Botswana. I knew their far villages, and most of them knew me. I was aware that when a Bushman had earned enough tobacco, in which commodity we paid them, he would disappear like a wraith. That they had no understanding of the employment contract didn't worry me overmuch, as there was always another in whatever rags to take the place of a tracker, in which capacity nobody on earth could equal them.

We used them mostly for tracking leopard, a difficult task if ever there was one. Usually it was repel-boarders time, as you could push a leopard just so far and he would charge. Far better if we were still able to bait them, hardly an unsporting practice. Yet the game department had gotten the idea in its mind that

Ju/Wasi Bushman.

Chips of ostrich shell are hand-drilled against a stone anvil to make beads.

this was somehow unsporting. I really don't know why, given that it was permissible in Zimbabwe, Mozambique, Zambia and other countries.

I have been told that a young male Bushman child was usually tested with a silver-dollar-sized tortoise that had twenty-four hours' lead. If the child was unable to track the tortoise—and very faint tracks it left, too—he went without food. Perhaps this is an old folks' tale, but somehow I don't think so. Certainly the Bushmen were trained to their life of hunting and gathering at a very early age. But I noticed even a couple of decades ago that there was some division of labor drifting into the Bushmen's existence. Some men were arrowmakers, and others did other tasks, with a clear division between hunters and all other adult males. All Bushmen could not track as well as the best.

Bushmen are probably the best-studied race in the realms

of anthropology and ethnology, far more work being done on them than on such folk as Eskimos, South American Indians or "lost" Phillipine tribes. We know that Bushmen painted rock overhangs with images of early Afrikaners and their wagons, yet, in a single voice, the Bushmen themselves say that they never painted and that such work came from an earlier people. Correct, but they were also Bushmen. That they are a separate race—despite great amounts of dilution with Bantu or black blood—is obvious in some. They are short, about five feet two inches being the average, are the color of dried apricots, and generally confound all rules of racial development by their oriental eye-folds, heart-shaped faces, and such features as steatopygia (i.e., the overdevelopment of fat on the buttocks to increase the body's fat-storage capabilities).

While I was on this safari, I had a curious conversation with a scientist who was studying the Bushmen. His primary chip on the shoulder was just who qualifies as a Bushman. That he worked for a charity or foundation that used the term "Bushman," I found a bit inconsistent. If, after all, tens of thousands of dollars were being raised for "bushmen," then I supposed the least the foundation could do was decide what they were in the first place.

For the purposes of this book, let's keep the definition simple, although possibly not scientifically correct. I say that a Bushman *looks* like a Bushman, speaks one of the Bushman tongues as his or her home language, and follows a life-style *when in the wild* similar to his or other Bushman groups. Of course, such things as clothing have long fallen by the wayside as a means of determining who is a Bushman and who is not, since today almost all Bushmen wear European or western clothes. The same would apply to the wildest of the !Kung working as a shepherd or cattle hand, although one of these is no less a Bushman than if he wore skins and beads exclusively.

The Ju/Wasi were probably the last of their kind to leave the old life behind because of external pressures. They still hunt with poisoned arrows and snares, but the fabric of their original life-style has become threadbare indeed. Perhaps you will realize why if we take a hard look at the Bushmen—or San, if you think there is some sort of racial slur—and see what has happened to them over the past thousand years and, in particular, over the past couple of years. . . .

The Bushmen are a diverse people who have become standardized through white and black ignorance. Their languages, "click"-based, are more or less individualized and only share the glottal smacks, clacks and other unique sounds in common. The Nguni-based languages of southern Africa, such as spoken by the Zulu, Xhosa, Shangaan, Ndebele and such tribes, also have at least three elemental sounds that the average European person would call "clicks." Yet, whether the ancient Bushmen had an influence on these black languages is still a guess, although it is probable.

The Bushmen were, and, to a certain degree, still are, hunters and gatherers, living off the land with "veld food" in the form of tubers, stalks and shoots as well as nuts and fruits, honey and larvae. Because game is generally scarce in the areas of Bushman habitation, they have had to become the great trackers that they are.

We have known about Bushmen for about a thousand years; much less in the West. Never very populous, the Bushmen as a whole fled before the advancing black tribes from the Congo Basin region and, for the last 350 years or so, from the additional enmity of the whites, until they have learned to live in desert and scrub places that neither whites nor blacks want or could make a living from. But, of course, there are river people who qualify as Bushmen, too.

Precisely where they come from, and how they fit into the physical and linguistic base of early Africa, is still not known, but they are considered the oldest people, remains of Bushmen having been found in strata aged at least thirty thousand years.

I think, without question, since they were not pastoralists themselves, they did not understand the concept of keeping domestic stock as did the whites and blacks, the keepers of stock viewing their herds as measures of wealth. To a Bushman, sticking a poisoned arrow into a prize bull or sheep was no different from giving a game animal the same treatment. I can, however, give no credence to the idea that the Bushmen did not understand what domestic stock was. These indigenous people of Namibia know every habit of the game animals and surely knew that a cow was not game. Still, domestic stock was fair game to these hunters, and certainly thousands of Bushmen have been killed since in retribution, hunted down as animals themselves and shot or speared to death, their children taken as household slaves by blacks and whites alike. In fact, the killing of Bushmen continued well into the third decade of this century.

Yet the Bushmen did not always come along quietly, as we shall see. When I was on the ranch *Gobabis*, on my earlier trip to Namibia in June of 1989, I was told that there was a cul-de-sac high up on one of the ranch's mountains that told a grim story dating back to German colonial days. I did not actually see the place myself, as I was having leg problems and it was at a considerable height.

There were two patrols of Germans, each seventeen strong, who were in the field to kill Bushmen for stock raiding. They needed water badly, and decided to use the small pool in a blind alley of rock, where a few Bushmen were waiting for them. Because there was only space for a single man to lead his horse, and the Germans were desperate with thirst, they were killed by poisoned arrows as they entered the enclave one by one. Nobody survived from the first patrol, because the colonists coming behind could not see what was happening to those who preceded them. Each one was killed as he entered the narrow space. But it was the only water within scores of miles, and soon the men were dead and several horses were eaten by the Bushmen.

Sure enough, the second patrol of the same strength came along, and they were also killed, although a couple, as legend has it, escaped the immediate trap to die of their poison doses a few hundred yards away. There were no Bushmen losses.

I suppose Bushmen always had the dirty end of the stick because they were "different," neither black nor white, which made them open-season game. Of course, they were less than babes in the woods when they held a cattle raid, their terrible arrow poison giving them a chance that was more than even, but it took a while to work, usually until the attackers wiped out the Bushmen.

Bushmen live in small family groups or clans that are loosely related. They were, at least historically, always on the move as they used up the slender foodstuffs of a particular area. They do not have traditional houses, but simple, temporary grass huts that provide shelter from the sun or, in the winter, from the cold of the desert. I was rather surprised to find that the Bushmen were quite careful of the heat, especially of the sand, as their feet would fry if they were barefoot during one of our long video sequences. They do have sandals—recently replaced by shoes and "tackies" (canvas basketball shoes)—but they usually didn't wear them. Why, I know not; that sand was nearly molten.

I was told by Volker that we were just a year or two too late to see the Bushmen in their traditional bush clothes—that starting in 1989 they had really gone for western cloth in a big way, rather than their usual leather. It was once decreed that women only wear duiker-skin aprons and that men only make quivers for their poisoned arrows out of camel thorn roots or "quiver-tree" limbs. The bushmen's interest in modern materials stemmed from their increased contact with the political groups seeking control of South-West Africa's future. Most of the able-bodied bushmen worked as trackers of terrorists (or freedom fighters, depending upon your viewpoint). The Bushmen had for the first time become important, since 1989 was an election year that would secure the country's independence from South Africa's mandate.

They were given any amount of pants and T-shirts emblazoned with political slogans because, in such a lightly populated country, every vote counted for SWAPO and DTA. As soon as the date of the election was determined (it took several days to count votes, so remote is some of the population), they were also given as much politically competing booze as they could hold, which wasn't very much. I don't like to use the American Indian as an example of very poor resistance to whiskey, but the result was similar. The way of life broke down.

The star of the movie *The Gods Must Be Crazy*, in a typical political T-shirt that reads "Viva D.T.A." (Democratic Turnhalle Alliance party).

In fact, it got so bad that distant tribes such as the Damara went to Bushmanland with actual traveling shebeens, and did very well indeed. One anthropologist totaled up the amount spent on an army payday at the single liquor store in Bushmanland, and found that those Bushmen employed by the South African Army would travel hundreds of miles to spend about the equivalent of eight thousand dollars, a couple of kings' ransoms in Bushmanland, on liquor. After I had been in the area a couple of weeks, it dawned on me that Volker Grellmann didn't have any Bushmen on his payroll, whereas he had had several the year before. Simple. They were not reliable for the fair but expensive prices he was charging his customers. He reverted to using blacks as trackers.

It seems to me that everybody wants to change the lifestyle of the Bushmen, usually for their own personal reasons. Bushmen in Bushmanland now have permanent water points powered by windmills, the shortage of water all year round being a direct reason for their old way of life. They are now somewhat reluctant cattle owners—or borrowers—and they seem to me not to water the stock but to leave it as much as possible to its ultimate fate of being eaten by a lion or leopard. I should have

Ju/Wasi Bushman.

42

Bushmen have the ability to "swell" with a reservoir of food, especially in the buttocks and thighs. But, as this picture shows, even the back skin is wrinkled in poor times.

said "killed" rather than "eaten," as the Bushmen, with hardly hidden smiles, happily eat the cat-killed carcass after shooing off the predators. I saw this several times during my stay.

Of course, having tasted the outside world, the Bushmen themselves are quite in favor of the new, easy life as opposed to the old. They have more children than they used to, and one wonders if it is because they have no television.

I am astonished except when I realize that not many people have been to Bushmanland, that I often hear of the Bushmens' wish to become more agrarian, growing crops as do the more sedentary tribes. Maybe certain people wish this were so, but as far as I have seen, it isn't. There are two large supposed agricultural plots adjoining Tsumkwe. Except for the fences to keep out hungry albeit sparse game, you would never guess that this

Ju/Wasi Bushmen.

was some sort of agricultural scheme. It has returned to the desert as surely as it was culled from its dry grasp.

I never saw *any* cultivated plants growing in Bushmanland that were planted or tended by Bushmen. A particular example sticks in my mind: Volker and his trackers followed a couple of bull elephants to the edge of a village. There was a water tank, which means it should have made no difference whether or not it was the dry or rainy season, but its tap was shut off. There was a garden patch about twenty by fifty feet that was apparently at one time planted with melons, but was now completely dry and dead. I don't think a drop of water had been given it in months, if not tens of months. It had been abandoned. What was worse, at least to my way of thinking, were the cattle, which were clearly dying of thirst, gathered around the tap from the water tank. That they were moaning fitfully aroused no sympathy from

44

Ju/Wasi Bushmen.

A rare attempt at teaching the Bushmen to become farmers. The top of the water tank has been crushed in by thirsty elephants.

the small village. Perhaps the people hoped that one would die of thirst so that it could be eaten with impunity. It was horrible. Naturally, we turned the valve and filled the trough.

I really don't know what the point is. But the Bushmanland I saw was pathetic and featured a people caught in the middle between a hunting-and-gathering culture and the modern world. I do not say that learning a bit of animal husbandry and agriculture would not be good for the Bushman way of life, yet I have seen the Bushmen continually written up and portrayed in ways that I know not to be true. They are no longer true hunters and gatherers, but they are not pastoralists or food-growers either. As for me, God spare me foundations and trusts. The Bushmen themselves do not yet know what they want to be, hunters, gatherers, farmers or pastoralists. The whiskey is good, and so is the food, now in relative abundance. Windmills are magic. But the Bushmen are not Bushmen very much anymore. They are a marooned people.

I have thought about this for certainly hundreds of hours. The only conclusion I can reach is that the Bushmen, unable to ignore its liquor and its water and its food, have been sucked into the modern world. I think we shall never see their like again. The Ju/Wasi were the last of the last. Now, because politics and anthropologists decree that they shall evermore wear cotton and eat off plastic, it is so. The cultural scientists and the politicians tell us this. But I think they never asked the Bushmen, who only wanted easy food, no matter where it came from. The Bushmen took the line of least resistance. Whether or not it was the fault of the "civilized" world to offer it remains to be seen. After all, who are we to say that they are not better off in the atomic age with their poisoned arrows and thirst?

CHAPTER
THREE

The author dictating notes inside his tent.

The first thing to do, after getting our equipment in shape, was to try to video Jerry Heiner taking a leopard. There were several baits already hung, but I thought a few more would not hurt, especially in a spot that I had a "feeling" about, near a water hole with a very nasty thicket next to it.

The tree where we hung the bait was a leaner, low enough for lions to reach up, but there was no sign of lions in the area. We took a particularly nasty-smelling knuckle of elephant from Jerry's trophy and wired it in place about eight feet off the ground.

I was still getting my sea legs from the weaving hunting car on the way back when we noticed hundreds of vultures, whitebacks, griffons and others, sitting on trees along our route. That they had not ganged a kill from lion, leopard, wild dog or hyena was evidence that whatever had made the kill was still busy on it. The first case of language barrier happened.

"Christ man, let's go see what's happening," I said to Gerhard as he almost passed the show by.

"No, we cannot," he replied.

"But why not?" I asked in no small agitation. Jerry had a lion license as well as a leopard permit.

Either Gerhard didn't tell me or he did not command enough English to do so, but I was able to get across that a lion had made a kill here, between the tall trees that were fairly rare in Bushmanland. He made a halfhearted swing of a figure-eight, but it was not until I got back to camp and had Arnold interpret that I realized that without a game department official in attendance, nothing, but nothing, was hunted.

I was irritated as hell, since I had gone through this drill elsewhere, especially in Ethiopia, but it took Volker a few days to make me understand. It was an old problem that stemmed from his early days in the northwest, when a client had taken— quite legally—a Kaokoveld elephant. But there had been such an outcry, from both misinformed and professionally ignorant people as well as the press, that his German clients had killed the Holy Grail, that Volker would never again be without a member of the game department present to say whether any game was not taken according to the licenses and rules. Even several years later, a couple of old ladies had cornered Anke and Volker in South Africa, believing the press and the professionally self-appointed "saviors" of the elephant rather than Volker. It would not happen again.

The Kaokoveld incident shook Volker and Anke, as they had several threats on their lives from do-gooders who didn't have the slightest understanding of modern elephant hunting and were under the impression from a venomous and hardly truthful press that all elephants were endangered, no matter what the professional conservation people said. Well, it sure sells papers. . . . Yet, if people were *really* in favor of the salvation of the elephant, you'd think they would trouble to find out the facts.

In any case, the house rules said that *only* if an official of the Department of Conservation and Wildlife was on board or accompanying the hunters would *any* animal be harvested. Thus, Jerry lost what might have been a good lion or leopard. The official was not with us, as we had just gone to hang baits. Such an error would not happen with me aboard again.

A very pleasant evening went by, and we went to check the baits again. Sure as hell, there had been a "hit" on my favorite bait, which was Gerhard's favorite also. I might point out, and certainly not to his detriment, that Gerhard had not had the good luck to take a leopard for his clients before. This was, I think, his second year as a professional hunter, and leopard luck doesn't come along that often, let alone a purely stupid cat such as the one we had been feeding.

Jerry Heiner had been on something like six safaris hunting leopards, and without a shot at all. Thus, at least in retrospect, I can see his point in not permitting Phil or Roger to risk his

Hanging a dead dog killed by a leopard, as well as an elephant knuckle.

bag through the sound made by their equipment. This would turn out to be a perfect setup.

Frankly, I was mad and disappointed when we returned to the bait and found the leopard lying just awakened from his gorging, half-asleep at the bottom of the bait tree. He bolted for the thicket but I bet Jerry a hundred dollars that he would at least have a shot that day, and within an hour and a half. He took the bet.

We returned to camp and got everybody who didn't have a better offer and returned to build a blind. The theory is that leopards can't count. Everybody milled around while we built the blind, chattering and laughing, but for my money that male leopard was watching the whole show from that thicket, where he had run upon being forced off the bait by our arrival. I could almost feel him watching us in confusion.

Perhaps it's Volker's idea, but all blinds are built by Anvo Safaris with a small tent as the central feature. Well, this was new to me. I was told that this would keep down the scent of man, but what's the difference when people climb up the very bait tree to hang meat? Surely there is plenty of human scent around, but when in Rome . . .

It took us about an hour to build the blind, and it was about two o'clock when it was finished. The tent was erected—a blob of imperviousness when the rest of the cover was semitransparent—but it worked! Carefully, Gerhard, Jerry and I slipped into the blind about fifty yards from the bait covered with grass and branches while the rest of the crew ganged on the other vehicle and went back to camp, singing and carrying on, and the chap from the game department drove about a thousand yards away.

It was like a Bessemer Process ironworks inside that tent. If I could describe the terrible heat, you wouldn't believe me. Jerry had Bam's .340 Weatherby, and I had the double. Gerhard had his 8-mm of whatever description. It was perhaps the hottest part of the day, around half past two, but we had not been there for a half hour when Gerhard's eyes grew round and he stammered in a whisper that the leopard was there!

We let it feed for a few minutes, already working out beforehand that I would lift Jerry's camouflaged cover when the animal was facing away from us, and give him a clear shot. I can see it clearly, a sinewy collection of rosettes that caught the sun perfectly. Slowly it turned its head toward us, and then swung it away. I eased the material away and squeezed Jerry's arm.

The .340 boomed and the leopard never twitched. It fell as dead as the nickel cup of coffee, the bullet precisely imprinted on its limp shoulder. Jerry had gotten his leopard.

I was both elated and dejected. What a *perfect* setup for a video! Jesus! We might have frightened him with the filming but I didn't think so. In any case, it was lost forever. Jerry had gotten his leopard—a fine male that edged the record book—

Jerry Heiner, Bushman hunter, and leopard.

but I had nothing from the best setup I had ever seen at a perfect hour of light. We went back to camp and took a lot of hero shots, but I had to come to terms with the fact that it was gone forever. It might be a full mount back in California, or even a head-mount with a rug. But it wouldn't be the ultimate trophy on video. I don't know whose was the greater loss, Jerry's or mine. I still think about it. . . .

We had gotten Jerry's elephant on tape, but not his leopard. There was to be no lion, although there were some about, especially a supposed completely black chap at the Nai-Nai Pan. Volker told me later that one of his professional hunters had had a "threat" charge from this male, but had not fired. When I asked him why, Volker said that the hunter had no lion license. I told Volker that this was certainly a case of obeying the game laws to a fault.

I was sorry that birds were not permitted on license, because, except for a slab of smoked kudu meat from Windhoek, I never tasted game the whole six weeks I was in Bushmanland. We had excellent pork chops, beefsteaks, chicken and other usual fare, but, as good as it was, this was not safari dining to me. If there was an antelope killed, as there had been by several of the European clients, it was invariably given to the Bushmen. I take this as generosity and a fair way to proclaim that whites were not taking their meat, but after all! There was no reason to have a restriction against shooting birds such as guinea fowl and francolin, but that was the rule. I got mighty tired of store-bought meat. The only change came when I killed an elephant and had a chance to eat a mouthful of the meat given to the Bushmen.

We spent the next few days along with Bam and Jerry, where we discovered that an ostrich nest had been found. The Bushmen made a traditional omelette by roasting the egg on coals in the sand with a fire, or at least flaming twigs, placed above it. The taste was not bad at all. It was done by heating the sand beneath until it was hot as Jesus, and then pouring the contents of the

Making an omelette of ostrich egg.

shell onto the hot sand and ringing it with burning branches. One would think it would be gritty and sandy, but it wasn't. After giving Bam the first piece and hearing her muffled words of approval, I tried some myself. Speaking of testing for poison, let me tell you about the Bushman arrows. . . .

An ostrich egg omelette.

CHAPTER
FOUR

A thicket of death—poisoned Bushman arrows.

Bushman arrows being more poisonous than any snake in the world, I was thrilled when I first had the chance to watch a Bushman and his nephew actually put poison on them. There has been a lot told about Bushman arrows and others, but I had better start at the beginning.

Some years ago, interested in the subject, I happened to research it. This was probably because of my love of blowguns or blowpipes, which such early author-heroes as Dan Mannix of the now-defunct *True* magazine used experimentally. I knew how to make curare (a strychnine-based poison used by various South American tribes), but I knew nothing of African poisons.

I once bought a series of blowguns from an American manufacturer who supplied a small phial of nicotine poison supposedly rendered down by boiling a quantity of commercial leaf insecticide, but I never used it. I improved on the darts supplied by using bicycle spoke wires, which were considerably thicker than the piano wire supplied in gross form by the makers, and got hold of a poison that I will not mention here, as it is not the stuff exactly recommended for a boisterous baby brother. The addition of plastic golf-tee butts made the darts fly very true, because the golf tees were aerodynamic and sealed the air from the "blow" perfectly.

Poisoning a metal-shaft dart involved using a binding agent to take the poison and hold it until it was needed. Toothpaste proved the perfect stuff, allowed to harden. The Bushmen use a sinew wrap below the point of the dart, but more of that to come. . . .

The use of poison on projectiles is nearly as old as piercing weapons themselves. The snake has always been known to be deadly, as the story of the Garden of Eden shows. Modern swords, broadhead arrows, and such kill by hemorrhage, not by poison. But if you're a little man out of reach of game, as were the Borneo Dyaks, the Jívaro Indians, the Guyanans and the Bushmen, the serpent was a friend, because it pointed the way to successful predatorship.

It has been said that the concept of archery began in imitation of the falcon: a feathered tail to keep the strike true, and a savage beak to kill the prey when it had fallen. Perhaps this is correct. The addition of poison came later, but not much, I think.

We do not know if Neanderthal man used poison, but it seems likely to me. Perhaps the Cro-Magnon did not; they were big enough as European sub-types that they could rely on hemorrhage. Yet no vestige of arrow or spear shafts of perishable wood remains to give us a hint. I don't think there is any doubt that, with the adder and cobra as tutors, mankind found early on that the use of poison could make him dangerous.

Of course, there are many kinds of poisons, either vegetable or animal, the latter being generally more effective. Usually, animal poison was of the type that would most readily break down animal tissue and either produce paralysis or runaway heart muscles while stifling the breathing of whatever animal or man got a dose. It was universally feared by those who came up against it.

There is a very old quote from a Zulu that pertains to the Bushmen at the time when the Zulu fought many skirmishes with them. Zulus fought standing up, originally throwing spears or assegais until they were taught by their great king, Shaka, to twist aside the protective shield of the enemy and stab with the short spear or *iklwa*, so named as it would make a sucking sound when the broad point was pulled out of an enemy. Yet the Bushmen, while they still had a stronghold in what became Zululand, brought fear:

"They are dreaded by men. They are not dreadful by the greatness of their stature, nor for appearing to be men. No, they have no appearance of men or greatness. They are little things that go beneath the grass and a man only feels [them] when he has been shot by an arrow. He looks but does not see the man who shot it. . . . They are fleas which are unseen from whence they came. Yet they tease a man. The bow by which they kill animals or men does not kill by itself alone. It kills [because] the head [of the arrow] is smeared with poison so that when it enters it causes a great deal of blood to flow. It runs from the whole body [from every orifice] and the man dies straightaway. This is the dreadfulness of the Bushmen and why they are dreaded."

Should you be knowledgeable of poisons, this is a classic example of the poison of an adder, such as the American varieties of rattlesnakes, in which the eyes, mouth, ears, and other body openings weep blood. Certainly it is a textbook account of the bite of *Bothrops atrox*, the fer-de-lance of Central and South America. Clearly, in the time period in which the Zulu was quoted, he dealt with Bushmen who used a great deal of snake poison in their mixture, rather than the grub poison used by the Bushmen further north. It was probably largely obtained from the African puff adder, *Bitis arietans*, whose bite produces symptoms similar to that of the fer-de-lance.

It may be that Bushmen have the oldest surviving poison used by man. What I cannot figure out is how they came across it. It wasn't obvious—far from it. It requires a hunter to dig well over a yard beneath certain trees to find the chrysalis of certain beetles. Yet, what sent the first Bushman hunter digging, when the larvae is itself benign? Almost all inventions have come from misadventure—such as Velcro, invented by a hunter who noticed that certain vegetable burrs were very difficult to remove from his clothing—so how did the Bushmen come up with a unique poison? Or *was* it unique? Did they get it from an earlier race? If so, who taught it to the earlier race? That somebody would figure it out is highly unlikely. Perhaps somebody had an ulcer and happened to eat the chrysalis of a very rare beetle, which he had to dig three or four feet to get, whose poison mixed with his bloodstream when such food is not on the menu and so far as we know never has been edible fare? How did the

Bushmen come up with it and not the wheel? Poison is far more sophisticated than any wheel. True, the South American and Mexican Indians built major pyramids, but they didn't have the wheel except for temple toys. I dunno. Any ideas?

My own fascination with poison (and I never thought I would have the chance to write about it) started with the second volume of a two-volume set of books, *Uncivilized Races of the World*. I have scoured the earth for Volume One, but so far without success. If you have one, please send it along and your wildest dreams will come true. Well, maybe not your wildest. . . .

In any case, I learned all about the Guyana Indians, who use curare on their arrow tips. The stuff is highly prized in heart medicine today. Don't ask me why. My doctor's number is busy.

The Borneo Dyaks also use a form of strychnine poisoning on their blowgun darts, at least according to Volume Two. What really fascinated me was that the Jívaro Indians of the Amazon watershed don't use poisoned darts for war! They use ordinary arrows (the blowgun not being used at all), which are familiar to me, since I've spent some time among such Brazilian Indians as the Tapirape and the Caiyepo. Don't forget that the Jívaro are the chaps who maintain a constant blood feud for the mere sake of the feud. Most have forgotten what it was all about anyway, but they still make shrunken heads of their enemies, known in their tongue as *tsantsa*.

I suppose an author is allowed a certain number of diversions from the text, the quantity of which are known only by his editor. As this seems to be one of the early ones, and the best way to read a book is for fun, let me tell you, as sort of an overview, about a couple of chaps who were caught by the Jívaro.

I remember being a fairly small boy the first time I saw these gentlemen, when my father took me to spend an afternoon in the Heye Foundation Museum of the American Indian. I always was a museum buff, because Father was president of the American Numismatic Society, although he specialized in military decorations rather than in coins—you know, medals, breast stars and such. In any case, the museum is on 180-something

Street, way uptown in New York City. I know it is still there because I went last year, despite a taxi fare that declared I had been to West Virginia.

They were still there, long hair and such, completely shrunken human beings about two and a half feet tall. For the first time I was able to get a guard to tell me who they were. One was an early Portuguese explorer and the other some sort of *garimpeiro* or gem hunter. Both were white. Now, shrunken heads were really something, but shrunken *people!* They were perfect except for the length of their hair, which was still long. Man, but I thought that I now knew it all! Shrunken people! Wow!

But nobody pays any attention. The Jívaro use repeated applications of heated sand to shrink heads into trophies after removing the bones. Imagine the job, if the trophy wasn't a head the size of a ripe orange to begin with. But they were perfect! You could even tell the features! I wondered about these men for years, but then puberty hit and I had other things to think about. . . .

On the basis that any knowledge may be useful, let me tell you how to make curare for fun, pleasure and profit. Not many books do. Yet, before giving instructions, let me also tell how effective it is on such as Grandpa and any recalcitrant school chums who do not toe the line.

I was able to find only one example of a man hit with a curare arrow. It happened among the Arawak Indians, and is recounted in a Mr. Waterton's *Wanderings.*

"His companion [the Arawak's] took a poisoned arrow and sent it at a red monkey in a tree above him. It was nearly a perpendicular shot. The arrow missed the monkey, and in the descent struck him in the arm, a little above the left elbow. He was convinced it was all over with him. 'I shall never,' said he to his companion, in a faltering voice, 'bend this bow again.' And having said that, he took off his little bamboo poison box which hung across his shoulder, and putting it, together with his bow and arrows, on the ground, he laid himself down close by them, bade his companion farewell, and never spoke more."

Surely, there is no known antidote or the stricken Arawak would have known of it.

To make curare, one must first find a *wourali* vine, in itself another name for curare, as is *oora*. That should make any poisoner happy. The South American genus is vinelike, about three inches in diameter and covered with gray, rough bark. It is not rare, but is hard to pick out of the vegetable miasma of the South American rain forest.

The Indians who make curare use a gathering basket called a *habbah* to hold sections of the vine of the *Strychnos toxifera* as well as a gathering of various juicy plants used as binders. One of the binders is called *hyarri* and is a strong fish poison used in pools of rivers. It is said that a square foot of *hyarri* will poison an acre of water. It does not affect the meat of the fish and probably works on the gills so they are paralyzed.

At this point, possibly because the Indians don't want to give away the secret of curare, they add snake fangs and poisonous ants to the mixture of the *wourali* and *hyarri* to throw off adventurous anthropologists. In fact, that it is a dodge was proved by analysis of a sample of curare which had no animal trace at all, just vegetable. Like Bushman poison, the curare is made well away from home, in the bush or the Indian jungle, for fear that youngsters might get into it and hurt themselves fatally in their play.

A sort of coffee is made with the initial pulverizing of the poison vine and *hyarri*, which is then boiled and simmered until only a black tar residue is left. This takes a while; more *wourali* juice is added, and the mixture is skimmed and cleansed. Curiously, a red pepper seed is added. If it revolves on its axis in the simmer, then the poison is not ready. Only when a seed remains stationary is the curare ready for darts or arrows. When it is finished, it is drained into a new pot and sealed with leather or sometimes large leaves. The poison made by the Macoushie people is considered the best, as it may have a secret ingredient, but ordinary curare is plenty powerful, paralyzing a monkey or a sloth in a matter of less than a minute.

Some tests of curare were carried out in England late in the last century and killed a hedgehog, although the poison had been made at least fifty years before. The hedgehog lasted a couple of minutes, but was unconscious from a rear leg scratch almost immediately. Some stuff, curare. Incidentally, it is often spelled *curari.*

Like certain East African poisons, curare is sensitive to heat, light and moisture, the efficacy of the drug being reduced if any of these agents is present. Therefore the tips of darts and arrows are carefully wrapped or otherwise covered when not in use.

The "big bow" men of the Liangulu people in Kenya also use a very virulent poison on their arrows when they hunt elephant. This stuff is made from rendering down the acocanthera tree or bush. A hunter tests a fresh batch by nicking his arm above the elbow and permitting a dribble of blood to flow down his forearm. When the blood is touched with the tip of a poisoned arrow, the stream rapidly turns black as it travels up the arm, and it is wiped away before it reaches the scratch. Surely this is no time for a pal to ask you if you've heard the latest joke; the speed with which the poison travels determines its deadliness.

In researching the subject of poison, I have found a favorite of both East African tribes and some non-Bushman people in Namibia to be the sap of the desert rose. Alas, no Linnaean Latin name was given, but there are so many sources that I am sure it is the desert rose that is used.

A favorite poison source is *Euphorbia candelabrum,* the candelabra euphorbia, which emits a sticky white sap when cut. Like South American poisons, it is also used to clean a pool of fish. C. J. Andersson, an early and very well known explorer of the great thirstlands of Botswana and Namibia, says that both the Hill Damaras and the Ovaherero tip their arrows with this poison, which is like diluted fresh latex. It is also very effective for use in water holes against large animals such as rhino and antelope. Curiously, it invariably kills the white rhinoceros and has no effect upon the black variety, *Diceros bicornis.*

In fact, I have noticed several references to so-called poisoned honey given to early explorers and bush hands that made them sick. Was this honey made by bees that visited the poisonous yellow flowers of the euphorbia?

The ultimate, however, is Bushman poison. Perhaps it does not kill as efficiently as curare, but it is far more painful. Let me give a couple of historical examples before I get into Bushman archery and poison. . . .

One of the most horrific stories that comes down to us is of a friend of the early missionary John Campbell, about a century and a half ago. His friend was hit in the shoulder by a poisoned Bushman arrow.

"We did everything for the poor wounded man in our power by cutting out the flesh all round the wound, administering *eau de luce,* and laudanum [tincture of opium] to mitigate the pain; but he lay groaning the whole night. At half past one, his pain was so great that we were obliged to halt . . . to lay him down under a bush from which he was never to rise. His appearance alarmed us, being greatly swelled, particularly about the head and throat. He said he felt the poison work downwards to his very toes, and then ascend in the same manner; as it ascended, his body swelled. He thought he felt the chief strength of the poison to lodge in one of his cheeks, and requested that the cheek might be cut off[!], which we did not comply with, persuaded that his whole frame was equally contaminated. The Bushman we had with us said in the morning that he would die immediately on the going down of the sun, which he certainly did; for the sun had not dipped beneath the horizon five minutes before he breathed his last. His countenance was frightful, being so disfigured by the swelling. On his brow was a swelling as large as a goose egg."

You can imagine—or perhaps you cannot—the agony of a wound that would make a man want to have his cheek cut off for relief.

Another description of death by Bushman poison is to be found in an 1873 book by C. J. Andersson, *The Lion and the Elephant,* a hunter's journal of Botswana and Namibia. There is an editors's note on pages 316 and 317 which refers to one Pereira, the head servant of an Anderson (although one wonders if there is not a typographical error and the name meant is Andersson). In any case, it reads as follows:

"This poor man, who was exceedingly well educated, speaking several languages, and who for a length of time was in the employ of Mr. Anderson, recently met his death in a very sad way. Several articles had been stolen from him by some Bushmen, whom he succeeded in capturing at the 'werft' [encampment] of their chief, and by the aid of some Damaras [also a Namibian tribe] was conveying to his waggon [sic]. Night, however, overtook the party half way, and Pereira, therefore, resolved to wait until morning before continuing his journey. He was followed, unobserved, by three Bushmen, friends of the captives, who shortly before daybreak crept stealthfully upon his place of bivouac, and by the light of the fire, alongside which he was sleeping, discharged three poisoned arrows at him. The first entered the left breast; he started up and seized his rifle, and whilst in the act of firing another [arrow] entered his arm close below the shoulder, causing him to drop his gun, and the next moment the third struck him in the stomach; but the latter alone did not penetrate. With the deadly shafts still embedded in the flesh, poor Pereira discharged his rifle at the murderers, who fled, and made their escape into the obscurity of the early morn. He then summoned the Damaras to his assistance. The arrow which entered the flesh of his arm was cut out, but the other, which entered the breast, and appeared to have passed around the blade-bone, could not be extracted. He was carried on a rude stretcher, hurriedly made for the purpose, to his 'velt-home' where he lingered in great agony for five days. 'The Bushmen's poison,' the narrator of poor Pereira's death goes on to say, 'is usually very fatal in its effects; but in this instance it had evidently become weak either from exposure or age. Otherwise [Pereira] would not have survived the fatal shafts for more than a few hours.' "

Bushman archery is singular to them, although some of its characteristics are not. A Bushman arrow head today is usually made from a length of fencing wire either bartered for or stolen, the head being flattened, very sharp and barbed, and the stem of the head measuring about four inches—in some cases less. Bushman arrows are segmented into four parts for very practical reasons. The point section is wrapped in sinew, which serves the same purpose as my old toothpaste-covered darts, the "holding" or "fixing" of the poison to the slick shaft. Of course, these are newer arrows, as we know that Bushman prisoners in Cape Town last century used a vegetable mastic or glue along with chips of stone or glass to act as the penetration medium, the point.

The head section of the arrow is sunk male/female into a joint of reed or heavy grass stem where it is bound lightly with another wrap of antelope sinew, to ensure that the arrow shaft will pull loose or break near the head rather than the whole arrow pulling out of an animal's body if it should rub against a tree or bush. There is a third "joint" of hardwood or bone, tapered to take the head joint and the main shaft. This usually falls away a short while after the hit. The fourth part of the arrow, the end, is not fletched with feathers or anything else. The nock is wrapped with sinew to keep the bowstring from splitting the arrow.

Although the poisoning of the head section is usually done by the archer or owner of the arrow himself, arrows are usually made by a specialist, which shows that a division of labor exists even in the most primitive societies. There is a great deal of difference in point sizes from different tribes and probably from different arrowmakers, the quivers I accumulated in the southern Kalahari having arrows with larger points than those of the Ju/Wasi, which are very small and fine, perhaps three or four taking up the space of a postage stamp. But the latter will still cut through hide or skin, and that is their main duty.

I have in my personal collection some bone-tipped arrows of the old style. These have conical points without barbs, although, except for the heads, the arrow shafts are identical to iron-pointed ones. Even though the fairly porous bone would probably hold poison, these are not poisoned on the tips, for safety reasons undoubtedly. The grub poison is always below the head, on the shaft, and on the bone points the poison is nowhere near the sharp tip, but lower on the bone shaft that forms the point.

That Bushmen are scared to death of arrow poison infiltrates their culture to an astounding degree. I supose, without risk of contradiction, that as each man has a method of doing in the next, death by poisoned arrow is extremely rare among the Ju/ Wasi. It has become less so recently, especially in drunken brawls, since the traveling shebeens have replaced the single liquor store in Tsumkwe. There have been several cases of women using poisoned arrows to commit suicide by jamming them into their thighs, but in the only case of this that occurred while I was in Bushmanland, the woman was saved due to quick incision. That the lady in question lived shows very clearly that Bushman poison of dried beetle larva juices has to melt in the bloodstream to be effective. It is not like cyanide gas or prussic acid, which works immediately through the moisture of the lungs.

The Bushmen use a very small bow, either because their tracking is so fine that they can get off a shot at no more than thirty yards, or because they don't go for a larger bow owing to their small stature. Let's face it: it doesn't take a big bee to sting you.

The bow is usually less than a yard from tip to tip, often very much smaller. It is bound with sinew at the bottom of the grip and sometimes at various stress points, the string being tightened by twisting the anchor point at the vertical top of the bow until it assumes a tone that, by experience, tells the Bush-man archer that it is properly tightened. It is generally made of raisinwood, which is not as springy as some of our Western woods but apparently does the job. The bowstring is double-twisted of the large sinews of gemsbok (oryx), kudu or roan.

I have shot a Bushman bow to considerably in excess of one hundred yards, yet the thing is made to get close-quarters results. I have told how the arrow is segmented, but I have not spoken of how the poison is prepared or applied.

Arnie got hold of a middle-aged Bushman and his nephew for our taped sequence. We shot the video in the sun-dappled

Author with Johnny and Petrus comparing Ovambo bow with Bushman bow. The bows act on different principles: only the Bushman arrow is poisoned.

shade, and it took some time, since a fire had to be lit first to dry the poison on the sinewed portions of the arrows. The making of the fire had all observers in stitches, as it did the Bushman himself. Basically, he could not make a fire because his nephew was too small to give proper friction to the spindle of hardwood that mated with a keyhole of very soft wood as a base. Twirl as they would, only once was some smoke forthcoming. Ever practical, I used the tip of a cigarette to provide final ignition—forgive me, all video viewers.

I hope I may also be excused if the Bushmen were clothed in what was their traditional garb until a few years ago. After all, who wants to watch a bunch of blue-jeans-and-T-shirt-clad aborigines chasing around? Of course, I had no idea of the problem when we arrived, but perhaps you will be so kind as to put it down to artistic license. After all, these are their own clothes; it's just that they don't get worn anymore, at least not very much.

Petrus playing the musical bow. When the Ju/Wasi hunter is going through thick cover in dangerous game country he will also strum upon his hunting bow so to give warning of his presence.

The author with Bushmen, trying to make a fire.

The problem, as always in nearly every culture, seems to be the *jeunesse*, the young who have no idea of the real state of things, but figure that they are experts, being of "student" age and younger. There is no discrimination on the basis of sex in Bushmanland, and very little pertaining to age. Thus, children made fun of their elders when they were wearing traditional bush clothes rather than the psychedelic shades of Birmingham. Personally, I wouldn't permit a vote on a government basis until the age of thirty, but then I am unreconstructed anyway. I plan to stay that way, incidentally.

While we went through the antics of making fire, I found out about the adult Bushman and his nephew. The boy's father had been killed in a drunken brawl about two years previously, and the uncle had taken the boy to raise. He was about eight or nine, and heaven knows what he thought of our video cameras and reflector boards. I surely must say the Bushmen are the finest natural actors that I ever saw. They never looked at the camera,

73

and performed naturally without any kind of self-consciousness.

The names of both uncle and nephew were /Cao. This could be Kao, !Cao, G'au or Ga/o depending upon how you heard it. It is a popular name among Bushmen, but without an anthropologist to tell us the errors of our ways in not spelling it with the greatest difficulty possible, to perhaps give their research more credence, I shall settle for the most pronounceable, i.e., Cow. In any case, they answered to the name as if it were correct.

We were at the point, past peals of laughter from the two Cows, when it was time to make arrow poison and put it on hunting arrows.

The elder Cow took out a container lined with wild cotton or some other cushioning material, and took from it several oblong chrysalises the size and shape of dried impala dung pellets. These contained the larvae of particular beetles the size of slightly elongated ladybugs. The larvae far outsized the adult beetles, of certain types that eat commiphora, marula and a few other tree leaves. When the beetles' eggs hatch, the larvae burrow straight down into the earth to a depth of from three to six feet, where they form a chrysalis that is the basis of the deadly arrow poison.

The first step in making the poison is, obviously, to open the chrysalis. The head of the grub is thrown in the fire, though I very much doubt that it bites. Next, the grub is carefully rolled between thumb and forefinger or massaged with a twig hard enough to rupture the internal organs. What remains is a bag formed by the outer skin containing the juices of the larva. When several grubs have been prepared this way, they are mashed together in the hip socket of a kudu or other large antelope until they form a liquid paste. Before any of the liquification of the grub is done, the preparer examines his hands for any minute cuts or abrasions, which could theoretically prove fatal if any of the liquid got into them, given the potency of the fresh grubs.

There is another curious angle to the northern Bushman poison. A "pirate" grub is reputed to kill and eat the larvae of the various arrow-poison beetles, and the poison from these

The beetle chrysalises used in making the deadly poison.

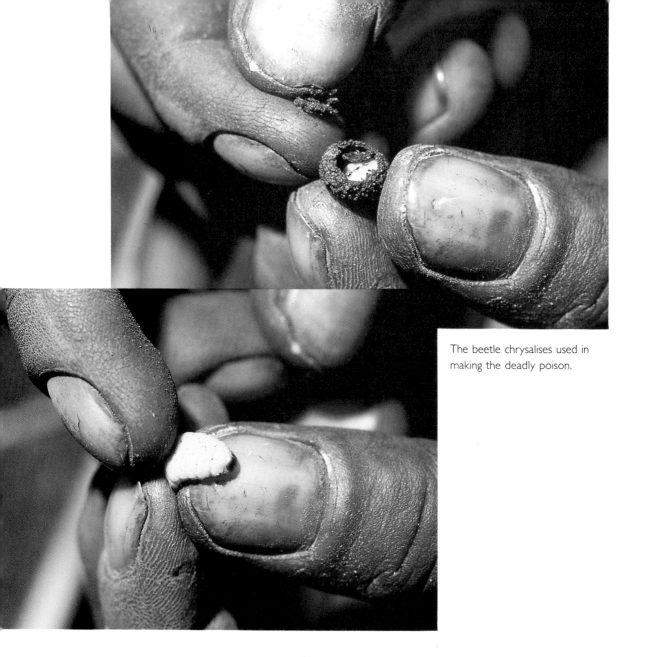

The beetle chrysalises used in making the deadly poison.

grubs is considered the best. The culprit is the *Lebistina* grub, and is highly prized.

While I'm at it, I might as well tell you that there is a

Mixing the grubs in the thigh-socket of a large antelope. If the grubs are too dry, a bit of aloe juice is added.

mysterious "white poison" in the form of a powder that is used to induce heart attack in various human enemies of Bushmen. I first heard of it from Volker Grellmann, who thoroughly believes in it as an agent for assassination. Apparently the powder takes several days to work, but it is infallible. Whether this is myth, legend or fact I do not know. . . .

Poison is placed on the sinewed part of the point, and dried by slight exposure to the fire's heat. It is never burned. Many layers of poison are used, each layer dried separately, and the finished product is obviously thicker than an untreated arrow headstem. In color it is rather like translucent wax, an amber that diffuses light. The arrows bought by tourists are free of the

77

Poison being applied to the sinew-wrapped shaft of an arrow.

poison for obvious reasons, but real arrows with poison may be acquired if one knows the right people.

There are two methods of putting the poison on the arrow, either using the grub itself after tearing off a front leg and smearing the body fluids on the arrow, or dipping a twig from the joint of the large antelope.

I have often wondered about the convention that places five—no more or less—arrows in a quiver made for tourists. When one buys an actual hunting set of bow and arrows, there should be a set of firemaking sticks, a stick with two blobs of mastic for repairing the bow or arrows, a digging stick (usually women are the diggers, but men also from time to time carry sticks), and a short spear that hangs from the quiver, with its own special scabbard. Sometimes I have found the hip socket of a large antelope, as well as a mixing stick to accompany it. There should be a fiber net, also, which is carried across the shoulders.

Not all the Bushmen use grub/larva poison. Their poisons are as different as their languages, although they seem to sound the same to a western ear. To the south, a mixture of snake, scorpion, centipede and other poison is used, but although quite deadly, these poisons are not reckoned to be as severe as that of the Ju/Wasi.

The spear in a Ju/Wasi quiver is almost never used to hunt with, but to finish off game that has already been hit and somewhat paralyzed by an arrow. The quiver, as I have said, is made either from the root of a camel thorn that has been baked overnight to release the bark from the pith, or from the traditional source, the quiver tree, which is split for its bark and then reinforced with sinew. Sometimes an unsplit piece is used if the branch is smooth enough. More and more I see quivers made from black plastic water pipe, which is ideal. However, it just lacks that bit of romance of the real thing. I'm sure the Ju/Wasi think that we buy bows and arrows to shoot game at home. How would you explain that a plastic water pipe was not superior for an archer as a quiver?

A very different Bushman product: the *guashi*, a musical instrument.

CHAPTER

FIVE

The fire that almost took the camp with it.

The first problem we had to face was that of batteries for the Betacam. It used them at an extraordinary rate, some eight a day of the nickel-cadmium rechargeable stuff. Filming had gone well, but it had to be somewhat curtailed for the reason that we just didn't have enough juice. We set up a recharging program at Tsumkwe, about twenty miles away, but by the time Roger was there and back, we had lost much of our early light. Perhaps the worst problem showed its Gorgonzola-cheese teeth the day we nearly lost the camp. . . .

It was lunchtime, too hot to hunt, and everybody except Phil, Angi and I was lying down. It first appeared as a small puff of smoke across a bush track that led to another village, the second-closest to us. Soon it was raging and screaming in the hot wind like a calliope gone mad, as heated air tore through the sparse trees and grass of the thousand-yard open space before us and directly upwind.

It was a fire, but what a fire. . . .

That it was traveling at perhaps thirty miles per hour meant we could do little about it. The tents were canvas. The dining hut and other enclosures were thatch. There was only one thing to do, swat it out when it came to the edges, and set counter-fires against it that we could handle.

Angi was the heroine of the day. She took a box of matches and put backfires in the holocaust's way. They would stop, she knew, at the right-angle road that came into camp, and she dodged through the flames in a way that made me afraid her blond hair would catch on fire.

Arnold saved the Department of Nature and Natural Re-

Klein Dobe during the fire.

sources camp some eight hundred yards away by cutting off the fire, but it was Angi who saved the camp.

Phil, a recently aroused Roger, and I tried to stem what we could, but it was too far and too close. In any case, Phil got some fine photos, although at the time I had not thought of them. Of course, as my friend through long association, Murphy, of Murphy's Law, was in camp, it looked as if the fire would take everything.

Bam and Jerry were asleep in the heat of the day, but mightily awake when the screams went up. The black gunbearers at first only turned over at the alarm because they thought we were going out early, and that clearly wasn't their employment contact. They resumed sleeping until they heard the word *mlilo*.

As the fire got closer, there were many people running here and there, doing essentially nothing. When we all saw that it was about to leave us with the likelihood of a gutted camp, we started getting photographic equipment together, as well as guns and baggage, to drag to the clear road that ran behind Klein Dobe. When the flames got within about fifty yards, Roger began to get ready. It was to be a colossal scene, perhaps the natural follow-up to *Gone With the Wind*'s burning of Atlanta. Waiting until the last minute to fill his viewfinder with flames, Roger started shooting.

His Betacam died a second later.

The rumor that I don't know any swear words is untrue. I said, "Golly! Shuckins! For heaven's sake!" I really let that fire have it, I can tell you. But it did not stop despite my epithets.

As the flames rose, I could only see Angi, bouncing around swatting with a wet blanket at stubborn areas of fire. Doug and Hanley were out hunting elephant on fly camp, just as well for them, though I reckon they saw the flames and smoke, but it was too late. They were fifty miles south. That's ten hours.

Jerry and Bam had most of their stuff out of the line of tents that marked their temporary habitation, but they had gotten into a hunting vehicle in which they were almost asphyxiated. Their stuff was safe, but I had to pour a very ample shot of vodka down Bam's throat before she got her bearings. The dark smoke and the billows of ash made it very hard to breathe, I can tell you, as can Phil.

Roger was sitting as if he had his only daughter in his hands, sort of rocking the Betacam. Then he came out of it and reviled the recalcitrant mechanism in a manner that we all thought appropriate.

Gone were our days of green and amber chaff of Bushman grass. All that remained were burned stubble and fire-hardened stems that were quite sufficient to pass completely through the sandals I wore when fooling with a couple of boomerangs that I had brought along. We were an emerald island in a sea of black, at least to the front of the camp. If Angi hadn't set her backfires when she did, I should be not at all surprised if we were found medium-rare to well done.

Of course, there were complications with the Betacam, which never seemed to have a simple explanation. It looked like the inside of a one-armed bandit when Roger took the cover off.

By this time we had received word that Hanley had, indeed, killed one hell of an elephant. I can only tell their tale as I preserved it via my tape recorder. It went like this:

Doug and Hanley, as well as their photographer, Glen Lambrecht, were worn out. But they decided to check a place that we called the Duck Pond, which was to the south by quite a few leagues from Tsumkwe. A casual glance showed nothing until it was determined by somebody that a very large elephant had drunk by walking on stones to get to the water, ostensibly so he would leave no spoor. Everybody was tired, and there was a

Klein Dobe after the fire.

question whether or not they would follow what spoor was available or head back to camp to relax after a long day. Hanley figured that maybe God had put the tracks there, and that they needed following. He had looked at more than two hundred elephants to date; why turn down Divine Luck?

Doug agreed to spoor the animal, which was unquestionably big and, judging from the state of its poorly digested droppings, very old. After a few miles of walking, the bull was seen by one of the trackers, and electricity began to crackle in the group. He *was* big, *really* big, and matched! Hanley loaded his .500/.465 double rifle and went along with Doug to where the elephant was loafing away the hot hours, which were almost finished.

Doug got Hanley into the stem of a broken-off bush and gave him the honor, a side brain shot that collapsed the bull into a cloud of dust. One shot. Glen videoed it very well, too. It was a bull that would last forever, well earned and well taken.

It was the next morning when we were told that Hanley had scored. We took Roger—the Betacam somehow having been fixed—as well as the rest of the crew. It *was* a big elephant, one tusk buried lip deep in the hard earth and the other a tantalization of perhaps The Prize, a hundred-pounder.

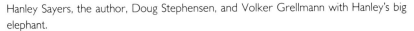

Hanley Sayers, the author, Doug Stephensen, and Volker Grellmann with Hanley's big elephant.

It didn't take long for the Bushmen to arrive to butcher the elephant, and they set to, on lines drawn with chalk by Arnold on the carcass. Which brings up an interesting phenomenon: Bushmen had never hunted or eaten elephant before in the region! A little thought made it clear why. Their arrows were much too small to penetrate elephant hide, and the poison too little to count on death, even if a venomous shaft were to get through. They had learned how to eat elephant from Volker, who, in his first season, took a couple of hundred pounds of elephant meat to various villages, ate a small amount to show it was not taboo or poison, and bingo, each time an elephant was killed, not a scrap was wasted. For nearly every Bushman it was the first time he had tasted elephant. This meant that all told almost seventy tons of meat were utilized by the Bushmen, probably quite a bit more than Volker and his group took themselves. This figure is arrived at by figuring that there were ten bull elephant on license and each weighed a minimum of about seven tons. Less trophies and blood, the total would approach seventy tons.

Rather than attempt to cut out the tusks on the spot, the skull and tusks were brought back to camp in a single load to let the sands do the job of extraction; even the most skilled skinner makes a few nicks with his panga or ax. The skull and tusks were buried to about five feet, and only the last client—which was me—had the tusks chopped out.

About six days went by before Hanley's tusks were unearthed. To my astonishment, they went ninety-four pounds a side, a truly fine jumbo. Hanley retired the .500/.465, never to kill another jumbo, in the same manner that a wineglass is broken so that it may never take a toast as fine as the last one.

We naturally had a celebration when Hanley got back that night, pulling all stops, including my harmonica, with which I assaulted the assembly. I'm not sure that Hanley and Doug Stephensen weren't sorry that they had killed the bull in the first place, if they had to put up with my talent.

I spent the next day in camp with Roger and Phil, mostly doing tape recordings of Bam and Jerry for this book. Jerry had taken what he came after, the leopard and the elephant (which went over eighty pounds a side, another fine tusker). He and Bam had largely relaxed over the last few days and were to leave in a day or so, therefore I figured I had best get their particulars, besides being old pals, before their due date came.

Jerry and Bam had been on four elephant hunts in 1988, all of which were successful. They had been to Zimbabwe, twice to South-West and then Mozambique, but their elephant with Volker this year was by far the best. Bam is a Florida girl, even though she has no accent, but then what do you expect from West Palm Beach?

Let's face it, hunting elephants is not cheap, which is very good for the elephants. Jerry found the wherewithal in real estate, especially in small apartments for employees of the gaming tables in Las Vegas, yet he got his start in the Northwest of America. I was quite surprised that he was part American Indian, and had inherited or was granted some timberland, which he sold for a start. For sure, he never looked back.

I have long thought that a safari was not composed of animals taken or even stalked. It is primarily made of hours spent about a campfire, making friends and enjoying nighttime Africa. I was proved correct with Jerry and Bam.

I can only now tell Bam that the day she and Jerry left, we passed up a boomslang—a deadly, back-fanged tree snake—and canceled the ticket of a black mamba. The boomslang was in the vines outside the kitchen and the mamba was in all its black-mouthed elegance just outside her tent. Bam has a horror of snakes, and I must say that they respected her feelings until she took the charter flight before they came out.

I have never seen as many snakes as the 1989 season offered in Botswana and Namibia. Lets see. . . .

The first snake I saw was heralded by a blast of Mick Arsenault's .375 H&H, neatly converting a very ample puff adder into a hatband. Later I saw another, as well as spoor or tracks of several, at the bottom of a cliff where I was hunting hyrax with my Bushman friend, Fritz. They were hunting the wood-chuck-like creatures, too.

The next exposure was Botswana, where Gordon Cundill and I had a perfect plethora of serpents in a couple of minutes. Gordon commenced the operation by using his twelve-gauge to blow a boomslang out of the roof of the dining hut at Chobe Camp during the Celebrity Safari, and we let one alone that was in the saplings about six yards away. Within a minute came an unnamed snake, perhaps a young mamba, that was killed by a rake wielded by the kitchen staff in the enclosure used for preparing food. And two more minutes hadn't passed when a fair black mamba—no question—was found in the same spot and executed by Gordon.

On the safari that forms this book, I have already mentioned the boomslang and the mamba that Bam missed—or perhaps they missed Bam—yet there were two more that got our attention.

The first was asleep in its most dangerous position, curled in a neat coil at the edge of a pickup truck's tire in the center of Tsumkwe while we were on the way to fly camp. Volker always carries a snake stick of reasonable length with a forked head, in case of such encounters. I remembered it, and we did a rather nice video segment on the snake and its horrors such as I have not seen in a hunting film before.

It was a very heavy puff adder, the snake that kills more people than any other in Africa. The thing that astonished me was the incredible speed of the strike. Whereas one could theoretically dodge a cobra, there was no way on earth that one could get out of the way of a puff adder when it had decided to bite. It was so fast that the vee of the stick was soaked with venom time after time as I failed to evade the strike, and my reflexes have not gone, yet.

Roger Olkowski was right when he said that to keep the snake would be "unprofessional." The vast, vast majority of adder bites happen when a man tries to handle a snake such as the puff adder. It can twist in its own skin and give a bite such as that received in Kenya by Alan Root, the famous wildlife photographer, while handling a baby or small puff adder. It twisted in his hand and he was bitten, as I remember, by a single fang. The poison rapidly spread to extravasation and turned his hand black, as shown in the photos in Visser and Chapman's book *Snakes and Snakebite,* published in 1978. Root was lucky to lose just his index finger to gangrene. Should you wish any photographs to keep you at home, by all means buy this book. . . .

Phil and Arnie Huber took the snake and smuggled it aboard the Toyota hunting car in less security than I would have. Since Roger did not know about their acquisition, the men were free to have Phil take the photo you see here and Arnold was free to fool with the snake as he chose, including showing fangs, etc. It was a very bad idea, but spawned some pictures that we would have not gotten otherwise, and nobody was hurt.

The second puff adder showed up in the thatched dining hut even before Phil and Roger got up at five o'clock in the morning to go to the game reserve to the north. Surely Phil, Arnold and Roger were within a couple of feet if not inches of it as it took refuge behind the wastebasket there in the dining hut. It was caught by one of the people cleaning up later, and kept in a wastebasket with a lid. Finally, Fifi and I decided that we would have it released a mile or so from camp rather than make Roger aware of its existence.

I always made sure that the end of the tent was severely zipped. I had never had any problems with snakebite besides burning down a toilet and a hut, and I was not about to. Incidentally, you can find the incident where I burned down the hut in *Death in the Long Grass* (New York: St. Martin's Press, 1990).

In my meanderings in 1989, I saw perhaps as many snakes in one season as in any other four or five seasons combined. It makes you wonder. . . .

While inquiring into the background of the Heiners, I was also able to get that of Volker and Anke as they arrived by car from Windhoek—a drive I would not attempt to make—a couple of

Puff adder (*Bitis arietans*) caught in Tsumkwe and taken on fly camp.

days before I was legally able to hunt. We had seen Jerry and Bam off on their charter, and Hanley Sayers, too.

Volker was a child in East Germany at the end of World War II. He, his parents and his family escaped to the West long before the wall was erected. Volker always wanted a home in Canada, with all those moose, but quickly changed his mind when he was offered Africa. Anke also came out to South-West Africa with her parents as a child. Volker has been a safari outfitter for something like twenty years in various parts of South-West/Namibia, and his and Anke's reputation got them the choice of the Caprivi Strip or Bushmanland from the government for a safari area.

We had before us some twenty days of safari. In my wanderings I had not cut elephant spoor yet, but it was because we were almost exclusively in the north, and the big bull elephants were in the south.

Elephants are funny critters. They work by a code of their own, without doubt, at least as far as I have seen. When I was hunting professionally in the 1975 season in Matetsi, Rhodesia,

Volker Grellmann.

we had them on license, but the latest dung we saw was at least three years old. I went back ten years later, and we had to almost weave our way between them. They were there in the thousands! I really don't know why, except that they may change territory when browse has been knocked down, and move to areas where this is not so. I have known this to happen in many parts of Africa.

I never saw an area that was so stratified as Bushmanland. To the north was the *only* place where cows and calves could be found, yet there were about one thousand bulls only in the southern country. Perhaps it was that roots and tubers were more populous in the south; yet I never saw anything but relatively old or even ancient bulls in the south of eastern Bushmanland. Never a cow or calf. Conversely, I never saw a bull in the north. It is not necessarily because of this dichotomy that Bushmanland

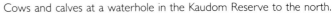

Cows and calves at a waterhole in the Kaudom Reserve to the north.

In the south, there were only bulls.

is an ideal place to hunt elephants, but it beats whatever is in second place.

In Volker's safari area there is a population of about a thousand bulls. Volker himself has wondered if the area is not some sort of geriatric gathering or old-age home, since most of the bulls are apparently beyond breeding and show little or no interest in the cow and calf herd in the Kaudom Reserve. Of course, the bulls are seasonal, usually appearing in the dry months and staying until the first rains. Then, as Hanley Sayers found out in May of 1989, even a small storm is enough to clear southern Bushmanland of elephant bulls. Hanley had hunted for about two weeks when an unseasonal rain fell. Overnight, the bulls were gone and he never saw another, although he had looked over something like a hundred of them before that freak rainstorm. He rebooked for September.

Southern Bushmanland, contrary to anthropomorphic feelings so high today, is an ideal place to illustrate the concept that conservation is the intelligent use of natural resources—in this case, elephants. Conservation is often confused with preservation, which dictates that natural resources may be put to *no* use but lie fallow without management. Happily, very few preservationists are raising cattle or growing corn as they would not harvest it at all but let it lie fallow. There has been a great deal said by preservationists about the so-called balance of nature, but such a balance has not existed since man drew the first squiggly line in the earth for seeds and tamed the first wolf, and certainly not since the first human baby was born.

Of the thousand bull elephants in present-day eastern Bushmanland, give or take a few, about a dozen were found dead each year before hunting started with Volker in 1988. They were dead of old age, a rare enough thing in this day of terrible poaching. Yet, given the vastness of Bushmanland, even the southern part, the seventy tons of meat represented as a gross figure of these dead elephants went to waste. Usually, if found at all, they were several days into putrefaction. Bushmen do eat some interesting fare, but rotting elephant is not on their menu.

When Volker and Anke came to Bushmanland with their safari business, they thought as much—or more—about the Bushmen as about the elephants. One of the staples of the Bushman's way of life is making original curios for a very elite market. These include beadwork, ostrich-egg-shell necklaces (to preserve the ostriches, Volker and Anke bring eggs from Windhoek for the market and let the Bushmen eat the contents, thereby saving wild nests), weapons and carvings of very high quality. The Bushmen are paid a good price for their work, too. The Grellmanns give a damn, and are fostering Bushman pride in their artifacts, which are a reliable source of income. Volker was granted a concession to take ten elephants per year, a little bit below the natural death rate. But it is the result that is really impressive. Bushmen get all the meat, and what they cannot carry is shipped off by Game Department vehicles to western Bushmanland, where there are a few people but no open water. There is a five-thousand-dollar fee to take an elephant, in foreign currency, and I am quite upset that it is currently paid into the general funds of Namibia; I feel it should be entirely given to Bushmanland, and it appears that it soon will be.

Thus, Bushmen receive the meat, Namibia receives a total of $50,000 in elephant licenses, taxidermists are paid to process the skin and ivory, there is a tourist market for Bushman crafts, and there is employment, at least for blacks and whites in the safari business. There was further employment for Bushmen while we made the video, since we needed subjects for the project.

The elephants? They're none the worse off. Volker makes it a rule that an elephant must be very old to be taken as a trophy, when they are past breeding, and I can assure you that very old elephants do not often have the biggest tusks. Usually they are broken, which makes taking a good jumbo a tough proposition.

Additionally, there are cooks, waiters, wood carriers, professional hunters and a host of other people who would not receive compensation were there not a safari business present that appreciates the real meaning of conservation.

Take your choice: elephants dying of old age and lost, or revenues, employment, sales of crafts and curios and other perks. I thought you would.

CHAPTER

SIX

Kudu bull, impala, and warthog.

Because elephants are where you find them, we saddled up the first morning just after dawn and started out, the sun catching the yellow of the dry grass. Phil, always protecting "Baby," his 600-mm lens, rode up front in Volker's Toyota with the big German, and Roger and I took the top of the vehicle. Of course, the view was superior to that below, but so was the heat, in unshaded, wind-whipped exposure. With Roger and me were Johnny and Jonas as well as several very malodorous elephant knuckles, which were left when the leg hide and sole were taken off.

As we had time on our side, the first thing we had to do was hang the knuckles up as leopard baits. We found likely spots and wired three in place with heavy four-gauge wire. We did not build blinds, waiting instead until we had a "hit" on the elephant meat. Even though leopards prefer fresh meat to carrion, they must find it first, and using rotten meat is the best way to make things happen. Of course, leopards will eat carrion if there is nothing better available, but their preference is reasonably fresh food.

Having hung the baits, we went looking for elephant and picked up a good spoor at a windmill pool northwest of camp. It looked to be a winner, but foot size doesn't have the tradition of indicating large tusks that it used to have in East Africa. In the latter, any elephant with large feet was tracked down and shot if it was big. It was only those with small feet and big tusks that survived. But, we were considering different elephants.

There are members of many gene pools and local races among Africa's elephants, and the biggest were without doubt the Bushmanland elephants that ranged upward into Angola and

Jonas climbing a windmill to spot elephants.

received a very substantial pummeling from guerrilla armies. The two largest ever shot—by body size—were both members of this group. They were both from this area and went over thirteen and fourteen feet respectively at the shoulder. These two were shot after 1950 and are listed in the Rowland Ward Records.

The tracks of this elephant were over twenty-four inches long on the round front pads. In tracking elephant, the criterion is always the front feet, which are circular, and never the hind feet, which are oval. For sure, this was an old bull, and he was alone. Obviously this was a spoor that we would follow.

I broke out the .470 Nitro from its soft case and, getting down from the vehicle with the greatest of care, stuck two long

A big jumbo walked down this road a few minutes ago.

cartridges in the chambers. Possibly one of the most dangerous places on safari is on top of a vehicle, as one must negotiate footholds blindly. I have had several bad spills when in a hurry, so I am never in a hurry anymore, and I don't load until I am on the ground. One of the worst such accidents took place in Argentina during my years there, and happened to a friend of mine, Amadeo "Chiche" Bilo. Chiche somehow caught his wedding band as well as his school ring, on the same finger, on a slightly projecting screw or bolt and hung there for several seconds while I lifted him off. The machismo of the Patagonian Desert did not permit him to cry out overly, but he had peeled

Another set of elephant tracks. Note the author's bootprint inside the periphery of the track and the fact that a leopard has also used the same road (*lower left*).

the flesh of the finger right down to the bone, and it was clumped like a ruffle at the end of the digit. Chiche didn't lose the finger, though I really don't know why. But then, he was a tough character anyway, killing a five-hundred-pound wild boar with a knife. You can find his story in *Death in a Lonely Land* (New York: St. Martin's Press, Inc., 1990).

I also stuck two panatella-sized cartridges between the fingers of my left hand and slid them up so that I was holding them about a quarter of an inch from their butts. The cartridge loops were full of solids, and except for a pair of soft points, so was my belt container. I do not go into what might prove to be combat without a goodly supply of rounds.

It was hot. Perhaps I don't mean *hot*, but I don't know how to express the heat of the day. It was forty-two degrees Centigrade or Celsius, take your choice, which was already 115 Fahrenheit in the shade. The trouble was there was no shade. It was about noon, but we all knew that it would get hotter until about three, when it would start to slide down again to perhaps a hundred degrees. Later it would shrink to the high eighties, but the trouble was that it was dead-dry heat. There was even a breeze, but perhaps that was the trouble. No sooner did a drop of sweat pop out than it was gone, evaporated, leaving a little ring of salt. By the end of the day spooring elephant, my bush shirt would stand up on its edge rather than crumpling to the floor of the tent,

Johnny and Jonas casting around for tracks at a waterhole.

which Phil thought very funny, rather like whistling in a grave-yard. I had already built a very professional layer of salt on my billed hat, sort of an expression of exertion, and I was professional small-boy proud of it. "Yes, ma'am, if you'd seen what these eyes have seen . . ." Anyway, after all that effort and sweat, I dropped it in the backwash of a motorboat while fishing the Chobe, and all the salt was rinsed out. That's what hunting is all about.

Johnny and Jonas took the lead, easily following the spoor, having committed it to memory. It is quite amazing to an outsider, but both Johnny and Jonas would from time to time leave the track and cut if off, so to speak, knowing instinctively where the bull had gone when he had stopped to snuffle in a patch of roots or tubers. They knew the spoor as surely as the FBI knows its fingerprints. Maybe an old scar, perhaps just a mark in one of the feet that was distinctive. Who knows? But it was within an hour that the men stopped and pointed to a great gray hulk as distinctive as a battleship on a golden sea of ripe grass.

Roger was filming us as we went forward over the three hundred yards that separated us from the elephant, and so was Phil. Christ, but he was big! Until I had spent more time afield in Bushmanland, I would have thought that lone bull was the biggest elephant I had ever seen! He was magnificent as we walked closer; we knew he really couldn't make us out beyond fifty yards or so unless he was farsighted. The ivory looked like toothpicks, so big was he by comparison, and I had to listen to Volker as he told me the real weight. His ivory would go in the sixty-five-pound class.

I was astonished, but the more I looked at the bull, the more I had to agree with Volker, as much of the ivory was hidden in the head, unlike other races of elephants, in which most of the weight comes from what is sticking out of the cheek.

I had a perfect chance for a side-brain shot if I had wanted it, but to run across a sixty-five-pounder on the first morning meant that we were bound to see one bigger than that in the nineteen days to come. At least I thought so. After all, a ninety-six-pounder was already in the barn, and the German client had actually had his *lunch* while deciding whether it was big enough to shoot! The elephant had been snoozing in the hot hours, a couple of hundred yards away.

Very hot and tired, and experiencing adrenaline letdown, we decided to have lunch here; there was a little bit of shade where the elephant had been browsing. After an hour, Johnny arrived with the Toyota and the goodies therein, not the least of which was water. We had drunk dry the entire three flax bags we were carrying.

That afternoon we looked in vain for more elephant spoor, but with no luck. We hung one more leopard bait, but decided to head south to the same area that Hanley and Doug had been hunting.

Our set-up at fly camp.

A "fly camp" on safari is no easy project, especially provided that it has not been provisioned beforehand. It is really a home away from home, with none of the relative luxuries of home base. All items of food and comfort must be taken from base camp and physically carried by supply truck to where the animal activity—especially elephants—is the heaviest.

We knew the morning was shot; it would take about four hours, maybe more, to get our proposed location, alongside a shallow flow of water that had not dried up yet. The truck was loaded and our camp head, Mateus, sent with it. Of course, we went first in case we should bump into a shootable elephant or hot spoor. In fact, it was during our trip to fly camp that we found the puff adder in Tsumkwe, as described earlier.

As usual, Roger and I traveled topside, with Phil and Volker inside the cab. The trip down was uneventful except for the puff adder, and we pulled up with slight difficulty on the edge of a large green pan. While camp was set up, Volker and I sat for the

Red-billed teal at the "Duck Pond" where Hanley Sayers picked up first spoor of his big elephant.

videos for a while, before Phil took off with his camera and Arnie to photograph the snake.

The area was beautiful, with low stands of hardwoods framing a large pan a couple of square miles in extent. Above, Bateleur eagles hung with their tailless grace, and flights of red-billed teal made me sad, as I was tired of bologna sandwiches. Of course, we would not have shot anyway, because there was considerable elephant sign even near camp.

There were also large, puffy cumulus clouds that made me as nervous as a parson in a cathouse. What if it rained again? Would we be out of business? What of the video? Dark thoughts ran through my mind. We had a small lunch of sandwiches brought from main camp, and while the day was still steaming—although not as hot as farther north—we set out to take a look around.

There was no doubt that here was where the elephants were. They had used the pan of water to slake their thirst at least every other day, and they weren't alone. Within a square yard I noticed the spoor of leopard, lion, kudu, gemsbok and duiker, quite a gathering.

The idea of leaving a fresh set of tire marks was more than coincidental; anything crossing our fresh spoor would have been there the night ahead, and as good as our trackers were, it isn't that easy to tell a print in soggy ground unless it is dead fresh and still leaking water into it.

After about two hours of driving around looking for elephants—which by all chances would be in the shade anyway, and we didn't want to spook them—we went back to camp and a most frustrated cook. No sooner had we left than three elephants had come by, almost knocking the tents down (according to the cook; in fact the elephants passed by five hundred yards or more), and had drunk at the pan. They all had teeth like white trees! But they had smelled the camp and retreated.

Well, I would rather agree with Volker that now there was enthusiasm rather than apathy on anybody's part. We had a look at the trio of bulls, now a few miles away, and there was nothing shootable. But it was the first group of males we had seen.

Kudu bull at a waterhole.

Returning to the fly camp, Volker, Phil, Roger, Arnie, the game guard and I sat down to a meal of bully beef and white bread, making a very fine lunch indeed. The beef was from Botswana, which has some of the best of corned products. Anyway, we were hungry. The morning's wanderings were thus far unfruitful—lots of fresh spoor, but nothing massive.

After lunch we took a short nap during the heat of the day. The wind was cooler here than up north, and it seemed only a couple of seconds after our heads had hit the pillows that Volker had us up. "Look at that!" he said, shaking me. I saw the rear end of an elephant disappear into some trees parallel with us along the water, maybe a thousand yards away.

"Any good?" I asked Volker.

"Can't tell. Only saw his arse. Maybe. Let's go and have a look."

It was less than a minute before we were bundled into the Toyota hunting car; Roger was especially keen to get some close-ups of a bull elephant. It was another couple of minutes before we reached the semi-open area where the bull had disappeared. Throttling down, we entered the parklike territory, expecting to spot the elephant any second. Johnny and Jonas were looking hard, but they hadn't picked up anything yet despite their ravens' eyes. Slower, now, the Toyota entered the sparse cover. No elephant. Nor was there ever to be an elephant. He had gone. Completely, utterly, he had gone. Neither Volker nor I believed it, but it was so. He must have heard the motor or caught the swirling wind and put on speed as we left the camp. The trackers hadn't bothered to track, since we thought he was close, and now it would do little good; the animal was clearly interested in putting a couple of zip codes between us. Finding the spoor, both Jonas and Johnny made gestures showing that the bull had well and truly shooed. Maybe he was the elephant of my dreams, maybe not. On the way back I thought of my old friend Mervyn Hallier, who had scored; my, but how he had scored. He had taken the elephant of his dreams. . . .

Mervyn had been a policeman in Tanganyika (now Tanzania) in the early fifties, and had as a good pal George Rushby, author of *No More the Tusker* and the subject of *The Hunter is Death*, by Tom Bulpin. Rushby, one of the top elephant hunters alive then, and a most skilled writer, had to leave the area, but told Merv about an elephant he had been after for years, a real whopper with tusks better than 130 pounds per side. Merv, whom I met at Kenton-on-Sea in South Africa long after he retired, killed the bull himself after a long and very scary hunt. The tusks went better than 140 pounds per side. *That* is a big elephant!

It is sneered at nowadays that civil servants of the Colonial Service of Britain augmented their salaries with two elephants per year on license, the ivory in those days selling for roughly a British pound sterling per pound of ivory. But this was forty years ago, when thousands of elephants were taken on control of agriculture alone. There was no overpopulation of people, the opposite being true. Elephants held the upper hand in agricultural terms, raiding native *shambas* or cultivated plots almost to the point of local starvation. I rather hope, as a former cropping officer, that nobody has the nerve a century from now to suggest that our approach was all wrong. If so, they did not see the ruined bushveld and hundreds of miles of smashed trees that elephant overpopulation brought. It is very safe for critics of culling to declare themselves correct with the longitude of time; but usually such pronouncements are wrong.

That afternoon, although there was a shower rigged in camp, and we had spent less than two days on "fly," we were going home. The reason was that Fiona and Anke would be arriving that evening, having driven from Windhoek. On our way out, we noticed that there had been considerable and violent elephant activity on and near a termite heap where we had stopped the evening before to let Phil and Roger photograph and video a magnificent baobab tree which was in direct line with the setting sun. Clearly the elephants did not overly favor our intrusion, as they had stamped flat the complete area where we had peed and relaxed on that termite heap. But there were no really big tracks, so we pushed on, arriving back at main camp at dark.

On the way we had stopped at an amazing place, clear proof

The author examining the old bore pipe where elephants put their trunks down to drink.

of the elephants' adaptability. This was called by Volker "the pipes," a couple of old water pipes about ten inches in diameter, the only remains of a bore hole or water point that perhaps had belonged to an old-time farmer. The pipes were worn shiny by the grit of elephants' trunks, showing that they often watered in this oasis of green ground. It is said that an elephant can smell water at fifty miles, and I have no doubt of this. This was a constant watering place, and even the grass around showed greener, not from the water, which was deep, but from their dung and maybe their urine.

The rumble and shudder of the Toyota was bound to end, and it did as the lights of camp came filtering through the twi-

The author's wife, Fifi.

light dusk. The first cheering thing was Anke's car, and then Fifi appeared, clean and grinning, at the edge of the hunting car. I had not seen her in a couple of weeks and, as usual, she was good to see.

I brought her up to date over a cold beer, and she told me of her drive all the way from Windhoek, where she had spent the night at the Kalahari Sands Hotel. Dinner was pork chops and excellent, and I took a long shower before piling onto the spring mattress and fresh sheets. Fifi told me of meeting Bam and Jerry at the hotel in Johannesburg, but I don't think she had finished when I fell asleep.

The next day was hot, and in addition to looking for elephant spoor, we had to check leopard baits. This was also part of my education. . . .

It was already hot at half past five, as we piled out for a shower. I used the electric razor for the first time in three days, and brushed my teeth until the gums bled. After a somewhat unusual breakfast of scrambled eggs, I commented on how excellent they were. It was all Anke could stand. "Ostrich egg," she said. "Fine, hey?"

Well, I must say it was the first time I had eaten ostrich egg for breakfast or any other meal. It was excellent, as fluffy as hens' eggs and with a superb flavor. The bacon was crisp as usual, and the sausages fine. I am not a coffee drinker, but the toast lent itself to the cold milk perfectly.

"We have to check the leopard baits today, but what do you want to do other than that?" asked Volker.

"Shoot a bloody hundred-pounder," I said, and took another toss of bacon.

I buckled on the cartridge belt with a holder of five .470 solids, the leather carrier given to me by Wade Brown of Dunn's Hunting Services. The Capstick African knife, which I had helped in a small way to design with Rob Charlton of Damascus USA, hung from the right side as I snugged on the belt. I put on the hat—sewn over the Hunters Africa logo was the International Professional Hunters badge—and pulled on the bill to make it secure. At least, I figured, I looked the part. . . .

Looking around the green tent, I was sure that all the paraphernalia was either dangling from my person or packed in my "possible" bag, a creation made some twenty-one years ago by cohorts of Peter Becker of Botswana Game Industries as their model for a shooting bag, the outside being elephant hide and the inside Cape buffalo.

Roger had chosen this moment to film the loading of the insulated food chests and other stuff. It looks smooth in the video, but I assure you that for some time I would have been pleased not to see Roger again, and as far as the food chests went . . . At last it was done, I am sure to the relief of Johnny and Jonas. The latter was clearly certain his day in Hollywood

Jonas, the local matinée idol.

was due, as he kept looking at the camera and flashing smiles the envy of anybody who had teeth.

At last we were on the main track, after having picked up the very tired game guard from the Department of Conservation. His dog, a large sort, would sooner or later be taken by a leopard, but I did not tell him this. Anyway, temporary companionship beats the hell out of being alone.

There was no hit at the first bait, the stark knuckles already in our nostrils before the tree was in view. But the second taught me a lot.

I thought I knew all about elephants and leopards, a fatal thought if ever there was one. Wrong. I had never used elephant meat in any form as a leopard bait before. There were complications, as in elephants.

I have always known, at least from my early African hunting days, that elephants are decidedly curious on passing remains of another elephant that has died, usually at the hands of poachers. Frankly, they are quite unnerving as they place a piece of branch or scatter some dirt over the body—or even bury their dead, as well as any human corpses. This has happened to sleeping humans, too, who were forced to "play dead" while the jumbo was around.

I have seen elephants take various parts of a carcass of their kind, especially bones or tusks, and carry them about in what was clearly a sort of ceremony. It is well known, too, that elephants will help a stricken one to stand and walk. There are too

A tree obliterated by an elephant.

many photos as well as the experience of hunters to pooh-pooh this.

But I didn't know what would happen if a piece of recently dead elephant were to end up as leopard bait.

Congruent with Volker's policy that all meat taken on safari was given to the Bushmen—this included antelopes and such—the only stuff left to bait leopards with were the skinner's scraps of elephant knuckles, the part left when other skin and such had been removed.

The second bait we visited was in a dense piece of cover, in a sausage tree at the edge. But what we saw was as interesting a piece of Africana as I have ever seen.

The tree was crushed flat by an elephant, large branches ripped off in a clear expression of rage. The elephant meat, such as it was, *had* been taken by a leopard that was lying at the base of the ruin as we pulled up; Johnny saw it. The damage to the tree was from the night before.

So this was why Volker insisted that I bring an elephant rifle as we "sat" leopard baits. Things could get Godalmighty nasty.

I was quite astonished until I had seen it a few times. Only where elephants were not present did elephant meat do as leopard bait.

We drove on with no attempt at rehanging the bait where it was, but put it in the back of the car for use as a new one. I thought it probably wouldn't work; whether I was correct remains to be seen, but we had no further visitors on it.

Along our route was a place also hit by a very big leopard, judging by his spoor. This was also the place where Bam had tried for a couple of afternoons, the heat insufferable in the tented enclosure, and without a show.

I felt, personally, that it was a no-go situation, since the leopard had, judging by his tracks, clearly checked out every tent-blind long before he had resumed his feeding. I by no means wanted to appear to contradict Volker's judgment. I was new to Bushmanland, that much was clear, but I felt that the open space to the blind's front of some forty yards would instill caution in a leopard. The blind was too visible with the tent as an understructure.

Still, we decided to sit the tent for several afternoons, all without reward. There were stupid leopards such as Jerry had shot, but they were not in the majority.

We ate lunch in the field that afternoon, on a neat folding table that Volker had brought and that was to be our usual seat. The big problem with Bushmanland is the distances that must be covered. This set me to thinking that Volker was not very expensive at all when the mileage was added in. Lilac-breasted rollers flitted here and there as we stopped by an old water hole or wallow that elephants had used, and we looked at a leopard blind that Volker had used to take a leopard in midafternoon for the first German clients. I wished it had been us. It was, again, a perfect setup for getting video pictures. I had run almost one hundred percent with clients who wanted a leopard, but the prospect seemed somewhat dimmer for me.

Roger videoed a fine whatchamacallit butterfly drinking up the slight moisture at the side of the mudhole and got some shots of Volker and me speaking of the great heights that elephants will reach to scratch themselves on the sides of trees. The rub-marks were at least fifteen feet high.

When we had finished lunch, we piled back into the Toyota, to hang more elephant knuckles and look for elephant spoor. Big stuff.

On the way, while we were looking for elephant tracks, Phil twisted around in the cab of the Toyota and shouted against the wind that we ought to demonstrate the power of the .470 Nitro for the camera as well as the video. It seemed like a good idea to me, as I had never done it. I asked him what he had in mind.

"Termite heaps, Cappy," he shouted back. "Termite heaps!"

Oh yes, he has a gift for such things. Duly, the car pulled up on the track opposite such mounds as were deemed appropriate. We got out and slithered down, the .470 being handed unloaded to me by Jonas.

It was quite a demonstration. I had decided to give Phil and

Roger Olkowski, the author, and Volker Grellmann looking at tusk marks about fifteen feet from the ground. A big elephant.

Testing the .470 Nitro Express against a termite heap.

Roger a countdown to the moment when I was going to fire; the voice would later be removed from the video. For the still camera it didn't matter.

I started out with a solid, non-expansion bullet such as was used against elephant. Even I was amazed when it blew a circular hole through the termite heap, sending billows of gray dust everywhere. Phil got it, and so did Roger. I followed the act with a soft-point, which made a huge crater, but the A-Square Lion Load, a bullet meant to turn itself inside out on impact, was the real performer. It created a cloud of dust as well as tearing off

the top of the termite heap in a blizzard of gray, compacted dirt. God, but it was impressive!

We hunted the rest of the day, seeing neither elephant nor anything else, for that matter, besides steinbok, an antelope that looks like an overstuffed fox terrier. There are slathers of them in Bushmanland, but not a great deal of other critters.

I stumbled into the firelight of camp declaring to all that I was a dead shot on termite hills, and were they on license? I had a cold beer and a hot shower, using probably all the hot water there was.

Fifi decided to come with us the next day, having sorted

out whatever women sort out. We rode three on the top, the center of gravity being breakfast. But this time we got some action.

We went first to a windmill not five hundred yards from the Nature Conservation camp, where Phil and Roger went crazy on sand grouse. These were the double-banded tribe; at any given second there must have been a couple of thousand, and there were perhaps fifty thousand in all that watered while we stared with protruding, bloodshot eyes.

There was also elephant spoor. Pretty decent stuff, as one

old bull was at least twenty-five and a half inches. They had milled around a bit and overstepped one another, but we thought there were at least a half-dozen.

Johnny and Jonas went forward through open country, spooring the bulls, as we followed in the hunting car. The bulls had stopped to feed fleetingly, and were probably in dense stuff by this hour as the sun ratcheted itself into the center of attention. Brother, it was hot! At least 115 degrees in the shade.

We went for perhaps three miles like this, Johnny and Jonas sorting out the spoor where individuals had wandered, when I saw a tiny flash of elephant, perhaps an ear, about two miles from us over the gently undulating terrain. We were getting down to the essence of the sport: expectation.

The steinbok.

We bailed out of the hunting car and loaded our rifles. Johnny and Jonas took the lead, still about two miles from the elephants. The wind was lying doggo, perhaps the worst situation for elephant hunting, since you couldn't tell when it would start up again, and from what direction.

We picked our way through mangled foliage and bulldozed earth as the bulls fed slowly along. They were out of sight now, as we were too low in the terrain to see them. There was no sign of the ivory.

Volker broke into a trot. The rest of us did, too, but it must have been sheer hell for Roger, who had a weighty battery belt as well as the Betacam itself, which tipped the scales at twenty-two pounds.

At last, about four miles from where we had left the car,

Double-banded sand grouse.

baggy behinds began to show about a hundred yards away. One was absolutely huge, as big an elephant as I have ever seen, at least a foot or so taller than the big one earlier with the sixty-five-pound ivory. At this point the wind started to blow again, a hot, dead-dry breeze that was at least from the correct direction, placing us downwind. The elephants were closer, but I was almost blown with the weight of the .470 Champlin-Famars.

We came up on the left of the herd, about forty yards away, and glassed them. There were several shootable bulls, had this been Zambia in the old days, but I still had hopes of eighty pounds or better, and I was looking for that huge chap, who was now on the right edge. I heard Roger cranking away with the video, and the discreet *cheeek-click!* of Phil's motor drive. I

Kudu bulls taken by Philip Kahl.

wondered abstractly why he had brought ten lenses if the 600 was always hooked up. Oh, well, photographers.

We paralleled the herd for a couple of hundred yards until Volker and I could both see the big fellow. One tusk looked very good, maybe eighty, but as we jockeyed for position, we saw that the other was broken. Dammit! Both Roger and Phil in the right position, the light right, everything perfect except for the tusks. I even had a sure side-brain shot. As we retraced to the car I thought, well, this is elephant hunting. We were back for lunch, not having gone more than twenty miles from camp. Angi rustled up the cook, who in turn rustled up a lovely selection of cold meats that we had with buttered bread and a couple of gallons of iced tea. In the afternoon, when things began to move

a bit, we would check leopard baits as well as look for that great kudu which had eluded me all these many years.

We didn't find that slimy sonofabitch of a kudu, which had followed me around Africa for a couple of decades. In fact, we didn't even check leopard baits. But at least I got lessons in how to prepare a proper snare for guinea fowl.

Perhaps Arnold, having spent so much time with the Ju/ Wasi, has developed their sixth sense. He had no way of knowing that we would be back that afternoon, but laid on three of the locals to make a snare from scratch. It was to turn out to be one of the most fascinating afternoons of my life.

I knew only one of the men, who had appeared in other sequences. It doesn't matter that they had a sense of sartorial splendor in reverse, as we asked them to wear the bush clothes of only a year or so before. They were still Bushmen, and hunters at that; considering that the old skills were on the wane, more is the shame.

Over the twenty-one years that I held various professional hunting licenses in four countries, I had trapped more partridge, which are known locally as francolin, of many different species, than the conservation authorities would have liked to know about.

Usually I used a simple loop with a sliding knot, and arranged the snare site like a funnel. My camps were never short of cold francolin for lunch—which is absolutely super—and a change from the sandwiches that are usual fare. Of course, we shot a few guinea fowl as well as francolin, but there were no shotgun pellets in the snared ones.

When I did *Peter Capstick's Africa: A Return to the Long Grass*, I hunted birds entirely in the old Matetsi area of Zimbabwe, either francolin or guinea fowl, and had the great pleasure of the work of two fine gunbearers, Alfred and Champion, grilling the lunch on open coals. As a Norwegian friend of mine, Chris Aall, would say, it would take a lot of that to kill you!

The Bushman snare was as unlikely as their poison. And it worked.

What amazed me was that of the four Bushmen, only one

Constructing the running knots of a guinea fowl snare.

The "trigger" twig of the snare.

The snare set and baited with a wild onion.

Close-up of bird snare showing wild onion bait and final "set."

knew *how* it worked, the oldest. The bush skills are going in a very large, economy-sized hurry.

As you will see from the photographs, the Bushman snare has a wonderfully sinister quality to it. It is as much innuendo as trap.

The first thing that they do is to select a whippy branch or stem from a live tree. Just any tree won't do, but there are many that will. Measuring from the point where the bent branch touches the ground, the Bushmen decide on where the first couple of feet of a bough should be dug in, the resistance of the soil making it necessary to "root" this part of the trigger firmly, well below the sand. The leafy end of the branch or tree is bent into

Death comes quickly from the snap of a snare.

a bow and buried, only a fraction of the middle of the bow show-ing above ground.

There is a form of wild sansevieria or aloe that has stringy fibers in the leaf. These are stripped over the edge of a digging stick, which is reasonably sharp, and the stringy fibers are rolled together over the thigh of a Bushman until there is enough to form a double-wrap, an immensely strong cord. I have tried it.

The cord is then fashioned first into a loop to hold the end of the springy branch, and subsequently into a trigger mechanism as well as the actual circle of twine that will tighten about the neck of a guinea fowl or a francolin.

The actual trap is set by means of a twig, sort of a Y shape on which there is a toggle, a part of the snare, which has a very small piece of wood or stiff grass injected. The loop of the snare that will catch the neck is kept open with small twigs placed in a circle. The ring or catching loop is under no pressure from the springy branch. The ingenious part is the trigger.

Taking the entire strain, the trigger is made by pressure on

The trip to the pot is just as quick as Bushmen stew the bird.

the small Y-shaped stick, one division of which holds a bait, usually a small wild onion (which you will recognize if you drink Gibson martinis), a favorite of both guinea fowl and francolin. The real ingenuity is in the relationship of the trigger and the snare.

The piece of cord that has the small piece of trigger tied in it is drawn to the buried bow. One end of it is placed *very* carefully against the bow, and the other end forms part of the trigger. The trigger is baited with the Y facing out, the bare trigger wood forming the other part of the sensitive "jam." The other small length of the trigger has the wild onion impaled on it.

When a game bird, whether it be a bustard, which may weigh thirty pounds, or a guinea fowl or a francolin, touches the wild onion, it disturbs the delicate balance of the snare and it goes off. Often the snare is set off by even the delicate touch of the setter, which immediately generates peals of laughter from his companions.

To my amazement, the snare worked the first time, overnight, when I was awakened by a guinea fowl at the first shadow of light. There had been an entire flock down to drink at the camp water hole, a small but ample source that was the only open water in several miles. One saw the wild onion and tried to grab it. Like the perfect mechanism it was, the loop snatched him off his feet and killed him in a few minutes. I screamed for Phil and Roger to get as many pictures as they could. They did! I wandered to the dining hut wondering why Bushmen were so small. If that snare was any example, they should have cholesterol problems!

The bird snare is also enlarged to handle such stuff as steinbok and duiker, though I did not see one set, and therefore have no access to the technicalities.

I might inject at this point that even such reserves as the Kruger National Park, in South Africa, do not tend to prosecute for instances of "subsistence poaching." It is not the bird snares that are the problem, not even so much those for smaller antelope. It is the savage modern snares, set by poachers, that take up thousands of yards of heavy-gauge wire nooses. These are checked every few weeks and permit large game to die, inch by inch, in agony. It is rather what oriental "long liner" boats are doing to big gamefish populations with their lengthy lines with thousands of hooks dangling on dripper lines off the main one.

CHAPTER

SEVEN

A Ju/Wasi woman. Looks are deceiving. She might be forty years old. Note the blue tatoos.

Several days had gone by in which we saw elephants that were shootable elsewhere but not in Bushmanland—certainly not since I had seen Hanley Sayers's trophy. Volker reckoned it was time that he made a supply trip to some Bushman villages, and I jumped at the chance to go with him, as did Roger and Phil.

Volker filled the back of the Toyota with tobacco, food and other stuff, but he knew as well as I did that the various political parties brought much more valuable fare: booze.

I had spent several weeks now with the Bushmen, and I kept myself from forming an opinion. There was no doubt that they were courteous, and their children the same. In fact, considering the western sense of privacy, they were much more open than I would have been if a race of white giants took to wandering through my home and that of my relatives.

But the day off was good in that it gave us a chance to speak, which we never really had when the primary topic of conversation was elephants.

Roger told me of an alarming incident he had seen when he was videoing the Heiners, when a Bushman actually fell off a truck as it was going full speed. One minute he was there and the next second he was gone as Roger turned to smile at him. He was motherless stoned on political whiskey, but none the worse for wear from the hard roadbed.

We visited some small villages that had a couple of cows that the lions had overlooked, but were otherwise unremarkable. The women, in particular, smoked tobacco in straight tubes made from either old cartridge cases with the rims removed or sections of bicycle handlebars.

The Ju/Wasi Bushmen no longer have traditional villages but use what they can of the civilized world in construction.

For the first time, Volker told me of a thing of which I was remotely aware, the intricacies of gift-giving among the Bushmen.

The Ju/Wasi, as well as other Bushmen, are the original egalitarian society for a couple of reasons: first, they have no tradition of fighting; in fact, they think bravery is stupid. This is reinforced by all their legends in which the winner is always the jackal, who gets the better of the lion by deceit, trickery or some other form of duplicity. Second, the Bushmen know that their only deadly weapon is the poisoned arrow, which has no antidote. They are a small and controlled people in terms of population and life-style, and can ill afford a death of any member of the band. Bushmen have the only non-jealous social pact of their race, and will go to incredible ends to see that no Bushman becomes jealous of another. The funny thing is that the Bushmen are reasonably jealous people. . . .

Let's say a hunter has been given a knife. A good one, too. Yet the receiver of the gift is aware of the small voices that mumble behind him about the knife he has, while the other men are poor and must use bone or stone or iron rather than the fine

The author playing with Bushman children.

steel. Sooner or later somebody will ask for the knife, and the hunter will give it, too, anxious to get out of the position of being an object of envy. In a phrase, everything is shared, from the smallest to the largest possession. Bushmen have, however, no large or heavy things in their lives. They are too small a people in stature, and they move about too much.

This applies to arrows and meat, too. Poisoned arrows are traded but mostly given among the Ju/Wasi. There is a complicated division of spoils among the hunters and their families, depending on who shot the first arrow that hit a head of game, whose arrow it was—perhaps it does not belong to the shooter—and such. Really, Bushman society is very complex.

Since we are speaking of poisoned arrows, I think I will mention a very antique letter that was up for auction recently at one of the international houses. Fifi noticed it in the catalog while she was attending the auction to increase our library of Africana for the sake of the reprint series. She cut it out. It is by Thomas Baines, the early explorer and painter who accompanied, among others, Livingstone. Dated September 21, 1865, it reads partially as follows:

"I send per railway the Bushman's arrow I promised. The head is now sheathed so as to turn the poisoned part inward. [This arrow was clearly equipped with a bone poisoned point that would reverse-sheath itself in the shaft.] If you draw it out and reverse it it will be ready for use, but you must be careful not to wound yourself as I believe the poison retains its strength. I must apologise for not having sent it sooner. . . ."

This note was three pages sent from Baines "At Mr. Wright's, 108 Brearley Street, Birmingham [England]."

We spent most of the day giving tobacco and the rest of the trade stuff to the Ju/Wasi, and Volker picked up a couple of artifacts that were waiting for him. He paid separately for these, and they had nothing to do with the gifts.

On the way back to camp, I was somehow able to get Phil to ride on top with "Baby" in its case, as I wanted to ask Volker about various interesting aspects of Bushman life. The first involved snakes.

Bushmen have gone bare-shanked except in the most recent times, and I was curious whether they were ever hit by the local cornucopia of mambas, puff adders and such that spent their time crawling around Bushmanland.

"Oh, yes," he said over the roar of the engine and the thump of the potholed road. "I know of three Bushmen who were struck. The first was a younger boy bitten by a black mamba, who died within a couple of hours of when he was hit." I repeated his comment into the tape recorder. "And then there was a woman who was supposed to be drowned by a python, but I don't have any particulars. I do believe that it happened, though. Take a big python and a small Bushman woman and it is entirely possible." Volker swerved to avoid a steinbok that wondered what in hell we were.

"I suppose the best-known case is from a hunter named Kwi, one of the men that Elisabeth Marshall Thomas, the anthropologist, wrote about. This guy was hit by a puff adder just below the knee, and although he didn't die, the leg turned gangrenous as most puff adder bites do, and he lost it. Just fell off. Oh, yes. They have their problems with snakes. In fact, you will never see a Ju/Wasi out of the village at night, or at least rarely. Afraid of snakes. Night is the time of snakes, with the heat. That's when they hunt. The Bushmen have no electric torches or flashlights to show the blue glimmer of snakes' eyes."

The next morning, Fifi decided to stay at camp to interview Anke while we went off to slay an elephant. We were about halfway through the safari now, and I had not yet begun to panic because of rain or elephants. For sure, a really great tusker would be behind the next tree; but I was increasingly thinking of that sixty-five-pounder the first day. Maybe we had misjudged him. . . . Maybe he would have gone eighty? He was a very big elephant, which made his ivory look smallish. That was it. He probably even had small tusk pulps or nerves. Why didn't I take him, that ninety-pounder? Maybe he would have gone a hundred?

I tossed on the soggy pillow until after midnight as that elephant grew in tusk weight. When I finally fell into fitful sleep, he was at least 160, perfectly matched, each side, maybe pushing 180 in the right light. If only . . . But I knew there was no use in exaggerating. He wouldn't go over 170 pounds per tusk— unless, of course, the left tusk was heavier. . . .

Fifi's tea came with the usual, fully pronounced "k-nock k-nock" as one of the staff brought it in. Another day. Jesus!

I reeled into the shower and let the water bring me to comatose life. The electric razor, working on rechargeable batteries— as if I hadn't had a lifetime of batteries with the Betamax video— sounded like a jet plane and my toothbrush like a band saw. But I made it to the dining hut in a photo finish with the platter of eggs and bacon and sausage and fried tomatoes and, oh, me.

I am told by reliable witnesses that I actually smiled, presumably with anticipation of another day of elephant hunting. I don't believe it, myself.

As usual, I strapped on the cartridge belt, filled the wowsie, Thorn Tree Café Elephant Gun Cartridge Loops on my bush jacket, and, with the .470 and the .375 Musgrave in tow, somehow climbed to the top of the truck without breaking my fifth vertebra.

We headed north because Volker drove us north. We picked up the game guard from the Conservation camp and after a few miles everything was fine. In the rattle of Afrikaans and KwaNyama I could have understood nothing anyway, but nodded sagely for the benefit of Roger, who could smear my African image if he really wanted to. My theory is to take no chances, so I muttered a garbled phrase now and then and even looked questioning. I also said, "Mmmmmuuuhh" a lot. This is a very safe thing to mutter, the years have taught me, as it sounds like neither acquiescence nor a violent negative. Believe me, nobody ever questions you when you say "Mmmmmuuuhh." You may find yourself alone more than you planned on, but it sure puts uppity Hollywood video men in their place.

Volker, clever chap that he is, had sent a pair of men from the base camp while we were in the fly camp to check a certain water hole near where Jerry had gotten his leopard. Sure as taxes, there were several elephants using it to drink just about every other night.

When we arrived at the windmill that supplied pump power to the shaft, Volker stopped the Toyota and wandered around like some sort of African Sherlock Holmes. So did I; after all, people were watching. I said, "Mmmmmuuuhh."

There were four elephants, all, of course, bulls, that drank either at dawn or dark at that particular pan. What Volker had in mind was standard practice, smoothing the ground so that we would know exactly when who was there in terms of elephants. Elephant hunting is not *all* walking; perhaps a bit of guile goes into it also. Doug was no longer with Hanley, as the latter had gone back to Tennessee, so he had kept an eye on the water holes as well as the leopard baits, a thing for which I thanked him, as I did in person. Doug Stephensen is a very fine hunter and he is also a very fine tracker. For sure, he knows leopards and elephants.

Our knowledge of insect and bird behavior meant that we knew precisely *when* various insects moved across the swept ground, as well as when the doves watered and the guinea fowl and francolin walked in. Each of these incursions on the swept ground would be like a red flag, but the flags would only go up if there were elephant spoor either on top of the bird and insect tracks or beneath them, which meant a night visit on the part of the big, gray hulks.

We checked the water hole for two days running, and it says a lot for the intelligence of elephants that there was no more drinking at this particular pan. They quit. Period.

Well, at least we knew where they *weren't!*

I had no idea—nor did anybody else—where these particular bulls went during the rains, or how far they wandered. I recall fingering a soft-point slug, probably a .375 H&H Magnum, that was cut out of Hanley's elephant's skull in an attempted side-brain shot, encased in gristle from a try a couple or several years before. I feel that since it was not a military bullet shot from an assault rifle—the *real* ones, not those so designated by the U.S.

Brushing the ground near a waterhole to be able to determine at what hour elephants drink.

Legislature—it was probably that of a farmer, since a professional hunter or even a poacher would know better than to try a soft-point for a brain shot, as it would not penetrate sufficiently. In any case, somebody had tried Hanley's elephant before. . . .

Because there seemed to be an increased activity of elephant in the northern areas, Volker and I decided to hunt in that direction. It is nothing for an elephant to put forty miles or so on the odometer over one night, and there was no question that we were seeing more tracks.

Perhaps the most interesting spoor was that of a very big fellow who was alone. It took us two days until we found out what he was all about, but his measurements sure fit the book!

We picked him up at dawn one day. He was walking the road. His dung, from retained warmth, showed that he was maybe six hours ahead of us, but that didn't bother Volker. We took the hunting car on the road, as long as the elephant had gone that way. If this seems unfair chase, please bear in mind that because of the age of the free-swinging spoor, we would never have attempted to follow him had we been on foot. Yet he stuck to the road, much as lions and leopards and other soft-footed game do; it is easier walking than in the thorns of the bush.

A whole day was spent on this doggone jumbo, and we picked up the tracks the next day, since he was big-footed and we had no more light. This little escapade also ended in a twelve-mile walk.

He had grown tusks like other elephants we had passed up—overnight, an orthodontist's dream. I awoke the second day when they approached 250 pounds a side.

Volker insisted that we have breakfast on the road this day, and I agreed with him. Every moment wasted would increase the lead of that indefatigable jumbo, and we were under way as the very first of false dawn broke, a very bad fingerpainting over the sere and sandy waste of the northern Kalahari.

We went like a branded cheetah along the spoor of yesterday. On a hunch, Johnny suggested that we take a track off to the side, cutting off several miles from where he felt the elephant's spoor led. Sure enough, it *did!*

But there was something peculiar about this elephant. He wanted to let us know that he knew that we were following him and didn't appreciate it very much. I was astonished. Far more than by casual chance, this elephant had broken trees—big ones in some cases—and carefully laid them *across* the track almost as a warning to us to lay off. It was far too much for coincidence, and I as well as Volker was impressed.

The joys of the car were left behind with the tracks of this elephant as he branched off into very thick bush. Volker thought we should see him soon, but it was seven miles by my reckoning before we did.

Ahead stood a giant baobab tree, I think you know the type, about as much as thirty men could encompass hand-to-hand. It was perhaps a mile off when we first saw it, given a slight rise in the ground.

"He'll be there," Volker whispered, and I agreed with him. It was the only shade in the bush, and wonderful cover for elephants to remember whatever they spend their time remembering. It was also a very long way through very hot bush. We had long ago eaten some sandwiches for breakfast, and we had already engulfed the offerings for lunch. In a stroke of brilliance, I called for a water break and to exchange the hot rounds for the .470 Nitro for fresh, reasonably cool rounds.

As we broke for my ersatz pause, I noticed a tree that really got my attention. There were fresh—*very* fresh—tusk marks one hell of a long way up. It had to be this elephant, and whereas we could not tell the size of the ivory, he was surely a whopper! I changed the cartridges and took a slurp of water, and we were off.

The stalk went according to the safari brochures. Volker led the way, in sure knowledge that the bull was under the baobab tree, and Fifi, Phil, and Roger took up the rear. After them came Johnny and also Jonas, grinning as usual, hoping that a Hollywood camera would irresistibly follow him. Volker was correct and, peripherally, so was I. There was a gray patch under the baobab that we stalked; we were aware at every second that the video was on us. We came to eighty yards in the fickle wind, then fifty and then thirty. At last we could see the elephant's ivory, at least one side of it. Sweat oozed like crude oil from my pores. Maybe there would be a charge from the hundred-pounder that we had so carefully stalked.

But Volker said a German word that I did not need translated although I usually confused it with the verb "to shoot." I looked through the little Leitz Trinovids at the ivory, but couldn't find it. Probably I couldn't find it because it was not there. The bull had broken off both probably fine tusks flush or not more than a few inches from his lip. Two days shot to hell from the viewpoint of an elephant killer, but they were two grand days as far as I was concerned. Either we wouldn't get an elephant or we would. Either we would get an elephant or we wouldn't. I had hunted enough to know the odds. A trophy is a trophy because the specimen is unusual for size and, perhaps, spread. A trophy isn't just a dead elephant.

The walk back to the Toyota seemed longer, somehow, and the sun more vicious and the air Venetian-glassblower hot. We all glugged some water and settled in for the long ride home.

About ten miles from base camp, there was a huge open

area, the sandy bush no more than waist-high. In it was an elephant, headed toward us. But we could see over the mile that
separated us from the big bull that the ivory was not exceptional.
That elephant walked within thirty yards of us, the wind being
what it was, blissfully unaware that we were there. But when
he had passed downwind, he put on a show of a mock charge
that none of us was sure wouldn't turn into the real thing at any
second. One of the big aspects of elephant hunting and observing
is to know whether an elephant is serious or not.

Almost without exception, any elephant will put on a fire-
works demonstration if you invade his space, caused by irritation
at having your face jammed into his, such as a southern European
might do to an Englishman.

An elephant bluff charge usually involves old *Loxodonta*

The bull elephant that almost walked into us.

staying in one place for the first couple of seconds and tossing his head so that the ears stand out and whip back and forth like a couple of sails in a sou'wester. He will then probably come forward a few steps toward you, still shaking his head, his trunk writhing around or held out before him. All the while, he will be making sounds like a steam calliope with all stops lashed down. This smorgasbord of noise is meant to confound and frighten you. It works.

At this point, Jumbo is not sure himself what he will do. He will either (a) continue his bluff, (b) go the opposite way or, (c) God help you, come for you in—believe me—dead earnest.

At least you will know when a real charge happens if you look for the following signs: the trunk will be rolled up under the chin, and usually, but not always, the ears will fold back against the skull as if they were plastered there. At that point it is permissible to run, especially if you are in bush country.

There is no stigma in running from charging elephants. I am *very* good at it. In fact, I took a silver medal in the last Olympics in that very subject. I failed to place in the lion-and-leopard category, but when it comes to elephants, I am rather talented.

The total concept of running from elephant charges is based upon wind direction, provided you have a couple of grass stalks or the odd bush or two to hide behind. Elephants don't see very well; they can spot motion at surprising distances, but mostly they work with the wind. If you are downwind of a jumbo, probably he won't find you, but if you give him your scent, he will be aware of exactly where you are up to a mile, maybe as much as two miles, away.

When an elephant charges, you'd better not get caught, the penalties being substantial if he means business. There were two cases of professional hunters paying the full price plus tax just last year. The first had herded his clients out of a dangerous situation with a herd or group and was completely surprised by a cow elephant himself. He was tusked through the chest and died instantly, the safety still on his rifle. The second fatal at-tack—both took place in Zimbabwe, the old Rhodesia—got the professional badly mangled although he was likely dead from the first couple of seconds on.

So what do you do if an elephant charges you for real? Besides "cutting" the wind on the elephant and disappearing into some bush if that commodity happens to be handy, the only way out is a heavy bullet above the brain, which may stun the critter with shock to the gray matter—but don't count on it unless he falls to the shot and you have time to get away.

Of course, killing the elephant works too, but it can be expensive. Most old bulls are more gentlemen than not, and don't give as high percentages of charges as females and young bulls. Thus, you are more likely to have to shoot an otherwise unshootable elephant in the tusk department, rather than be charged by a fellow that fits in Rowland Ward's dreams. *My* dreams are of being charged by something over two hundred pounds a tusk, which is as unlikely a circumstance as my dreams themselves.

Incidentally, various game and conservation departments are less sympathetic with hunters who have to kill small or female elephants. Their view is that the hunter had no business being there in the first place, let alone provoking an attack.

The miles disappeared under Volker's tires—excuse me, tyres—and we stopped for a break to hunt rabbits. Ladies pick daisies, just like the old stagecoach jargon for an imminent stop for nature's call. I was again able to talk Phil out of the lower berth, and I joined a sweating and dusty Volker and asked him to tell me more stories of Bushmen.

He chuckled over recalling one of his first experiences on coming to Bushmanland, which involved a slightly wounded kudu. The antelope was hit a slight crease across the breastbone by a client when Volker still used Bushman trackers and there was no political situation to think of. The hunting party followed it the whole day and took up the track the next morning, when the bull kudu joined with a herd of females and young. Smelling a miss or a very slight hit, Volker asked the opinion of the Bushmen, who were still full of energy, knowing they would get the meat.

The one of the party who could speak some compound-fractured Afrikaans replied that the kudu would die any moment, as blood had been drawn. After another five hours, Volker realized that the Bushmen thought he used poisoned bullets, like their arrows! I got him to repeat the story for the video, and it came out well.

The next morning we took two vehicles. One was to check leopard baits and the other to take Phil, Arnie, Roger and me to a huge and famous baobab that had several century-old engravings on it and was a landmark for some early *Voortrekkers* or Afrikaners who took all their possessions north to get away from the British domination of the Cape Colony of the times. It was a wonderful tree composed of a very strange set of branches for

Lunch next to a famous and huge baobab tree.

Baobab bark is similar to the skin of an elephant. This bark was engraved by remote travelers more than a century ago. This tree may have taken root at the time of Christ or before.

a baobab. The Bushmen say that this tree is writhing in agony from being stuck with a porcupine quill when it was young. I have no idea how old it is, but that it may have been a sapling at the time of the birth of Christ doesn't seem unlikely. Maybe it only dates back to Charlemagne. . . .

There are hardwood pegs leading up the soft, pithy trunk, which show that Bushmen who are long forgotten used to raid the honey that the upper branches protected with their height. Probably these are the twentieth or fiftieth set of pegs, given the age of the tree.

For some reason, elephants don't seem ever to have damaged baobab trees in Bushmanland. There is no reason to think that elephants are new to Bushmanland, sort of a political result of the Border and Angolan bush wars, so I find this curious. In Botswana, which is better watered, as well as in Zimbabwe and Zambia, which are virtually oceans compared to Bushmanland, elephants are a major contributor to the falling and death of baobabs. Perhaps there is some reason for this that will only be known to the scientists of the future. Beats me.

Roger set up while Phil took various photos of the different types of bark on the tree. Some were smooth, and other areas were pimpled or corrugated. Roger was finally ready with the Betacam, and took a couple of cassettes of me pontificating on elephants. I was even surprised myself as I became a bit tight-throated when we got to the people I have known who were killed by elephant. I suppose a couple of incidents like that never completely leave one's memory.

In the late afternoon, Volker and Doug Stephensen came by in the other car, having looked for elephant spoor and checked the leopard baits. Since we were only about ten or twelve miles from camp, I rode back with Volker and Roger, while Phil took the other car with Arnold and went to check another bait. It's too bad that Phil wasn't with us, because quite a rare thing happened, and we were in on it from near the start.

Not more than a mile and a half from camp, the small encampment of Bushmen near Klein Dobe had found a very large beehive in the base of an old termite heap. It wasn't twenty-five yards from the road, and we were as surprised to see it as the Bushmen probably were not.

Bushmen usually find honey through their children, except for rather obvious hives. If a bee, laden with pollen, is seen making literally a beeline for the hive, he is followed until he is out of sight. Then the youngster takes a sight on the next passing member of the hive, and so on until it is found. As we stopped the vehicle, the first huge slabs of honey and grubs were being removed by a very old man whom I had not seen before. It was fascinating fare.

The old fellow was bare-chested and halfway down the excavation that had been made. The members of the hive, many thousands, I suppose, were clustered on a small, almost naked tree a few yards away, the swarm a solid object that would have most Americans terrified after watching some "killer bee" movies. Yet they made no attempt to move against either the Bushmen or us. Roger was in his element, running through a couple of cassettes of video.

Why they didn't attack us and were downright complacent was beyond me. They sure were much tamer than even the sweet-tempered Italian strain of honeybees, even running down the tattered shorts of the old man without stinging. Oh, yeah, there were a few stings as children swatted at the host, but nothing compared to the mass death that lurked in that bare tree.

The honey was magnificent, combs as big as serving platters, each probably weighing ten or more pounds. There were a total of six of them by the time the Bushmen were finished.

What really got my attention was a microcosm of the Bushman philosophy toward every form of wildlife: they didn't take all the combs, but left two huge ones in place, so that the hive would not be depleted. Perhaps they had taken honey from this hive for generations; I didn't know, nor could we get the question across in pidgin Afrikaans. But the hive would stay where it was because the bees had some reason to stay: at least thirty or forty pounds of honey and grubs.

Here was the classic case for the conservationist. Use wisely, but do not totally deplete. Today it is a sophisticated thought to all but hunters. What a thrill it gave me to find it was also an ancient and practical concept!

It is said that one doesn't really have an African book unless there is some mention of the greater or lesser honeyguides to show that you know your stuff. Well, I have a story, too.

It happened in Botswana when I was writing *Peter Capstick's Africa* on a 1985 trip. I suspect if you have this book, you already know about the honeyguide bird, but let me refresh your memory if you don't remember. . . .

There are six varieties of honeyguides, the most common being the Greater and Lesser. They range throughout southern Africa, and some species are represented in most of the sub-Saharan areas of woodland. The honeyguide is quite unique in its symbiotic relationship with both man and the ratel or honey badger; it will actually guide man or animal to a hive by leading the way with its agitated calls. It will stop at various trees within sight of its more powerful ally, and call until it is followed.

Naturally, such behavior is considered spooky by most primitive peoples—and I don't think this leaves professional hunters out. There are all sorts of legends concerning what will happen to a man who shortchanges the honeyguide by not leaving some bee grubs for it to eat, along with a bit of wax from the comb. The most common tale is that next time the bird will lead a cheater to a poisonous snake or a dangerous animal as revenge if it is not given its stipend.

I have not seen honeyguides more than a half-dozen times, but when I've had time to follow them through curiosity, they have invariably led me and my bush help to honey. But this one in Botswana, in the Chobe region where I was hunting with Gordon Cundill, either had been cheated at some time in the past or was having a bit of fun with us.

Gordon first noticed the excited cries of the Lesser honeyguide and suggested that we follow it, which we did. It flitted ahead, but the trackers and gunbearers grew increasingly nervous as the cover became thicker. Within a couple of hundred yards it was heavy riverine bush, but still the small bird led us on. At this point I was starting to get a bit of activity from my ancestral hackles, too. Certainly this was not beehive cover, as *zinyosi* preferred the more open areas where close bush did not interfere with direct flight. There were whites of eyes showing as we went on, following the chittering, and they weren't all native eyes.

Finally, my double rifle held ready, I noticed that the honey-guide had stopped and was silent. It was sure a great place to find a pride of lions lying up to get away from the heat; maybe an old buffalo or a leopard. I eased forward a couple of quiet steps when an outline appeared and was instantly covered with the ivory bead of the .470 Nitro Express. But what was it? In the murk I couldn't see it well enough, but it was getting bigger as it took a step or two toward me. I felt the adrenaline start to pump, and glanced to my sides. No place to go if there was a charge. I was hemmed in. . . .

As quietly as goosedown, a female kudu eased her head through a green bush and spotted me at five yards at the same time I saw her. She swapped ends and exploded out the other side of the cover as I took a great breath of relief, my first in what seemed several minutes.

Now, the question is why did that damned honeyguide go to all the trouble of leading us here, right up to halitosis range of an animal? Was it confused and maybe thought the lone kudu cow—very unusual to find one alone, in any case—was a dangerous animal? Had it been cheated by a honey hunter that it had led before, and was trying to get even? I know the term "birdbrain" isn't very flattering, but the honeyguide had already proved that it could think logically and with anticipation, as it most clearly led us to the exact spot where an animal was. Was there something to the old African stories? Usually, except for religious fables, African tales are rooted in fact.

I really wondered as a few nervous laughs from the staff began. I decided to have a look further. Maybe the kudu cow, sound asleep if we could approach so closely, was being stalked by a lion or leopard. Maybe there was a beehive nearby. Was it simply coincidence? Gordon had the men fan out to see if they could find anything. Nothing. No beehive, although who knows whether there had been a leopard stalking the kudu? There was too much vegetation and fallen, damp leaves to be certain if a lightweight cat had been easing up on the kudu, but we didn't know for sure.

It was just one of those instances that cause me to reassess how much I know about Africa and its creatures. . . .

It was quite late in the afternoon when we arrived back at Klein Dobe Camp, but early enough to get some work done. I had yet to tape Doug Stephensen, and figured this was the ideal time to do the deed.

Doug is as brown as biltong, of average height and with hair the color of mine quite a long time ago, the sort of stuff that you don't miss overly if it thins. An orphan, he has seen some hard times, but made the best of it. He can track with the best, and I would be quite at ease anytime he was at my side, even though he uses a .458 Magnum, which is not much of a gun in my opinion, based upon rather serious usage. Doug, with a face that is sensitive, brown-eyed and the color of a badly polished boot, is a good hunter. I watched him.

Doug hunts in the reverse season in the Central African Republic. He was born in Ndola, in what became Zambia, in the late forties. The first really big influence of his hunting life was Stuart Campbell, a very old friend of mine from Zambian days, while Doug and he were in Livingstone, just across the Victoria Falls from Zimbabwe, on the Zambian side. Doug met Stuart at Lusaka, the capital, in the company of Johnny Uys, who was killed by an elephant about the same year, 1969, that I got to Zambia myself. Stuart Campbell (and let nobody tell you that professional hunting is not a small world) was responsible for Doug's start in photographic safaris. The great Andrew MacLagen, himself born in Zambia, between Lakes Mweru and Bangweulu, began Doug's apprenticeship on dangerous game. Andrew, since dead of leukemia, was schooled in Scotland and decided on an army career with the Black Watch. However, for reasons best known to himself, Andrew became a power-line

Doug Stephensen.

surveyor back in Zambia, and later was one of the first men
employed by my old competition, Zambia Safaris, when I worked
for Luangwa Safaris Ltd.

Doug Stephensen was with a family in the Belgian Congo
and went through a portion of the uprising there. He doesn't
remember much of it except that it was very confusing until he
ended up in a home/school in Kenya. In fact, he is not sure why
he was taken to a Kenyan orphanage except that the authorities

thought perhaps there were relatives of his in-country, some-where near Nyere, where the home was.

Doug was in the orphanage until he was thirteen, and then he ran away. He wanted to go back to Ndola, to some people he had stayed with as a nipper, some very kind folk. The youth hitchhiked through Kenya and Tanzania with black truck-drivers, because they would ask the least questions, yet he was careful to leave his ride whenever a border post was ahead, cut-ting through the bush to avoid it. Fortunately there was quite a bit of water, and Doug lived on handouts from the truck drivers and whatever he could find. Finally he made the Zambian border with Tanzania, although it was still the Northern Rhodesia bor-der at the time. Doug says he was so careful that it took him three months to make the trip. He spent several weeks at an old road construction camp about seven hundred kilometers (a bit over four hundred miles) from Ndola, his destination. As Doug was walking warily down the road, what attracted his attention was a big green area among the trees, which turned out to be a semi-wild pumpkin patch. To a very hungry boy of thirteen, that meant food. He remembers looking around to find something to cook the vegetables in. He found a couple of old paraffin (kerosene) tins. There was a stream nearby, and Doug stayed about a month, eating boiled pumpkins. He will never forget the taste. . . .

At last the pumpkins ran out, and Doug hit the road again, making Kaperi, and then the rest of the way to Ndola was fairly easy. Doug looked around and found the family he was looking for, but, fearing kidnapping charges, they had to notify the au-thorities. Doug was taken into custody and placed in a secondary school. Of course, the future professional hunter hated it, and he ran away again. This time he went south and, having turned fourteen, got a job with a construction company in Lusaka. Doug started at the bottom of the ladder as a "spanner boy," in main-tenance of the company's fleet of vehicles. The experience stood him in good stead as a professional hunter; he can pull a piston or find a problem with the best of 'em. It was while a spanner boy that he met professional hunter and elephant expert Johnny Uys. The rest is hunting history.

CHAPTER

EIGHT

Sunset silhouetting a baobab tree.

Having worn our feet off to the mid-knee region, I thought it might be appropriate if we "sat" a couple of leopard baits and then continued the elephant hunt, allowing things a couple of days to calm down.

There were two leopards open for business, one a long way north that looked like a female to me, and a very big male about ten miles from camp. We opted for the latter.

Since the scene that starts this book occurs at night, I had better explain the unique theory of Bushmanland and its "problem animals." When a client books a safari in Bushmanland with Volker Grellmann, he signs a separate agreement to hunt "problem animals" at a much-reduced trophy fee, kills counted separately from the normal safari bag. This policy is intended to reduce predation by lions and leopards on cattle that have been "lent" to the Ju/Wasi by a local foundation. The deal seems to be that the Bushmen may keep any offspring, but the adult cattle are what might be called a "trainer" course in animal husbandry, which is not in the Bushman bag of tricks. In my opinion (and not only mine), the scheme has not worked, as the livestock has been decimated. My views on Bushmen as stock herders I have given before. They seem valid to me, but of course there are other views equally valid and based on a greater familiarity with the Ju/Wasi than I can claim.

Problem animals may be hunted by day or by night, but the use of artificial light is not permitted, the logic of which somehow evades me. One would think that a cattle- or horse-killing lion or leopard would be fair game in a control (nonsporting) context under any basis. Nope. Even though the anthropologists and ethnologists quartered in Bushmanland decree through the

Department of Nature Conservation that a particular animal is a "problem," it must still be killed in a "sporting" manner. Further, a game guard or other personnel from the department must be with a hunter of "problem" game.

The leopard we were hunting was not a problem animal, so he might be hunted—correctly, as far as I am concerned—only until a half hour after sunset. Doug and Arnie had seen to the building of a blind big enough to accommodate four people; Volker, Roger, Phil, and me. The question was, first, whether there would be enough light to record the end of a leopard, and, second, whether there would be too much noise from the cameras, video and SLR Nikon, to get any shots.

I saw a film a few years ago in which a dead leopard was worked with monofilament nylon to fake a real shot, and I would never be a part of it. Either it's the real stuff or we don't offer it in the videos.

We had lunch after another morning with the elephants, and there was no need to forgo the ice-cold beer, as we sweated much more than we peed. At about two-thirty, Volker got the team together and we went off to the leopard blind. On the way we decided that Roger's Betacam was quiet enough not to disrupt the cat at some fifty yards, but Phil was only to snap his motor drive after a shot had been fired. We sent Roger into the blind first to take the right side, and Phil, Volker, and I followed him. It was hot. It was too hot even to speak of, and we needed no reminders.

There was a slight breeze blowing from the bait to us, which made the afternoon one to remember with the smell of rotten elephant knuckles. A freshly skinned piece of elephant foot hung alongside the fetid fang-and-claw-torn original bait. Flies the size of clay pigeons swarmed us, which sort of interested me, since there was much more succulent fare in the branch of that tree. But perhaps we smelled worse, given the heat.

The seconds crawled by like slugs with terminal athlete's foot. Even the birds were silent, resting in the shade like any creature with a modicum of common sense. There was a shaft of copper sunlight on the fresh bait, which had been placed that morning, and I watched it move with the tiniest arc as the white sun swung toward the west. Jesus, It was hot! I was soaked with my own juices.

Funny about leopard blinds—I guess it is expectation. It seemed that every time I looked at the bait I could see a massive, transparent leopard hunched there, looking around with amber eyes, a symphony in dappled gold and black. But there was nothing.

Slowly the ball of sun slid down, changing imperceptibly from white to brass to pinkish as it nestled in the bushveld at what seemed not a hundred yards away. Here is where I'll confess, I was not a believer. I hadn't thought that a leopard would cross the dead open area in front of the blind, especially since his tracks showed that he always came down the road behind us late at night. I was right. As the last light faded, a half hour from the time when Phil or Roger could photograph, Volker nudged me with a sour face. Nope. No go. No leopard. Let's go home. It was okay with me.

We gathered up the express rifles in case of elephants, the shotguns in case of wounded leopards, and whisked the .375 Musgrave off its forked-stick perch and removed its camouflage wrappings. Supper sounded good.

It was. An Angi-inspired chicken dish, it was excellent, or maybe I was that hungry. The dumplings were smooth and as tasty as the white wine, the latter chilled to perfection. I had held off from my shower rather than cramp the supper, but immediately after I had sidestepped puff adders and mambas to the canvas enclosure at the rear of our tent, I thoroughly splashed.

Tea came at about five o'clock the next morning, far too early for anyone but hunters. Volker had had a dream that strangely coincided with mine, that we would find a good elephant that day. To hell with the leopards. We would go back to the bastinado, the flaming delight, heat that would make a shish kebab blanch—the tracking of elephants. After all, it was what we were here for. . . .

The sun was just threatening us as we drove out of camp, the same poker-red disk that we had seen in the leopard blind the day before. The thick lower atmosphere enlarged it as it came unstuck of the horizon, and I saw how primitive peoples were persuaded to worship it. In a way I did, too.

Volker, as usual, was at the wheel, and Fifi was up top with Roger Olkowski and me. The air was still cool and clear, a morning that made you wonder why you went home when the safari was over. A lilac-eared finch flitted over the car, close enough to catch in an open hand, and the world was wild with the calling of gray and yellow-billed hornbills. A steinbok darted across the track and I saw a funny, predatory look in the faces of Johnny and Jonas. The cool dust enveloped us as we stopped by the conservation camp and took on our policeman for the day. Every day of this was unique. I was elephant hunting.

There were once-green cushions over the board that formed a seat above the driver's cab, but they had seen greener days. The most comfortable position was to stand up, developing sea legs as the Toyota pitched and tossed along the uneven ruts of the track. In no time, one learned the necessary apprehension for the next bump and wallow, during a long safari developing forearms as if one had spent the time in a gym.

The bush was greenish and grayish, a bewildering, out-of-focus streak that endlessly ran on below my vision, the yellow shooting glasses picking up a smooth layer of dust that I knew better than to smear with a handkerchief. They were never the same once you cleaned them.

Unconsciously I checked the cartridge holder for the .470 Nitro solids and also thumbed the loops at my left breast. Full. I was loaded for elephant, literally.

The night before, I had cleaned the Champlin-Famars double, getting about a third of Bushmanland out of the twin barrels. The problem was that I had not had a chance to foul the barrels from the necessary oil and nitro solvent, and I knew that the first shots would be quite high, unless I put a couple of rounds through the chambers first to vaporize the oil and the residue of the cleaning products that I had used.

I looked carefully for elephants and noted that the wind was in our faces when I asked Volker to stop while I popped a couple of caps. Clambering down from the rear, I took the unloaded .470 Nitro from Jonas, dropped two of the long cartridges into the chambers, and clicked it closed with a solid snap that would have made George Caswell of Champlin Firearms very happy. Looking around for a target, I settled on the top of a termite heap, since the previous test had impressed me very much. It was about sixty yards away and I held several inches low to allow for the clean, slightly oiled barrel. *Wuuump!* went the first barrel, a bit high, but I had allowed for that. *Wooom!* went the left, and the tip of the termite heap disappeared. I knew better than to glance at those still in the car. It was impressive and did wonders for their belief that maybe I could hit an elephant, but I grumbled my way to the top again. "Maybe a whisker left," I said, with a harrumph! "But, I suppose it'll have to do." I was delighted.

It was elephant moving day. We cut spoor after spoor only to find that they had not stopped to feed but had gone on in different directions. Damned if I know why, but we couldn't close with any of the big bulls whose tracks we found. And, they were reasonably fresh. I knew it wasn't my shots as I had been fifteen miles away and they haven't yet produced an elephant that can hear *that* far!

The day was fruitless. Volker drove into the hangar where the Toyota lived when off duty, and we all piled out. I had a couple of cold ones while Fifi used the shower and was then able to scrub myself into Bowery acceptance while there was time for another cold one before dinner. I didn't know what had happened. Neither did Volker nor Johnny or Jonas. But, maybe there would be some elephants tomorrow where there were none today.

The author glassing for elephants.

CHAPTER

NINE

Guinea fowl feathers where a lynx has killed.

We had nearly given up on the two leopards that were feeding. One reason was that we were out of bait because Jerry Heiner's elephant knuckles had gotten too ripe; they had an aroma that would give a maggot crossed eyes. Also, after four afternoons of sitting in blinds in which the heat would have cashed in a vulcanologist, the leopards seemed to have more sense than we did, obviously snoring away the afternoons rather than feeding. Vultures could not reach the baits, so there was no reason not to feed at night. I know that we did. . . .

I know. First prize is a week in the northern Kalahari Desert in October. Second prize is a month. It had even gotten hotter than late September and early October, but for elephant hunting it was ideal. The bulls would have to gather under some cover rather than keep moving and feeding all day. This gave us a chance to catch up with them.

The morning of the eighteenth started out with Arnie delivering one chameleon, which was promptly dubbed Edgar, after an old friend who saw all things, especially future moves on a backgammon board. Edgar wasn't one of those throwback chameleons with three horns like a Triceratops had (or the monstrous *griffs* from Burroughs's Tarzan series for that matter); he was a proper chameleon who'd been caught stealing flies next to the skinning shed, where he probably had a better life than ever before. He was positively bloated. Phil Kahl put him in a rather bare tree after we had a chance to interview him, and he disappeared in the low, gray branches like I would not have believed. The only way to find him—and we *knew* he was there—was for one of us to go to the other side of the low tree and get his attention, whereupon the other guy would see him edge around a branch in an evasive tactic. He was absolutely the color of the bark, too, and only his very slow movement gave him away if you were looking for it. He had not only immense varieties of colors—he once turned a bright blue to match a wastebasket lining—but his stealth was extraordinary.

Edgar's gait was one step back and two forward, the strange, rocking movement allowing him to approach his prey like a windblown leaf. After all, ever try to sneak up on a fly?

The Africans were scared dungless of him, too. The chameleon is the heavy hitter in a dozen tales of the bush, the most common of these being that he entered into a race with a *leguaan* (monitor lizard) at God's insistence. The monitor was to carry the message that Man must die, and the chameleon the opposite, that Man need never die. I don't need to tell you who won.

The other story is that the chameleon knows absolute truth and can spot a thief a couple of miles away. The reason is its

Edgar the chameleon.

independent eyes, which, even to me, are spooky. At any rate, Edgar lived in the tree outside Phil's tent for the duration of the safari. I finally took him home to South Africa and released him in a bottlebrush tree and was unable to find him again. I like to think he is still there, possibly with another (we didn't know what sex he or she was), which he well might be.

After breakfast, I got a real fright. From nowhere, great puffy clouds with bases covered in tar appeared. Cumulonimbus. At least my university course in geography (yeah, I thought it was about places rather than meteorology, which it turned out to be) made me remember. The trouble was that they contained rain. I remembered what had happened to Hanley Sayers when all the elephants "bombshelled" for greener places. Maybe it would happen again.

But Volker wasn't upset. Whatever rain did fall fell in the concession area rather than to the east in Botswana. If anything, we stood as good a chance of drawing elephants to the area as losing them as pans of water filled up from the deluge.

The south, about ten miles from Tsumkwe, got a pretty good soaking, and several times we had to scrunch under the slick tarpaulin used to cover equipment. Fifi was a good sport because, as she wisely reckoned, her hair was a lost battle anyway. She tied a scarf around her tresses and said, firmly, to hell with it.

Volker and I had decided to put the leopards on hold until we killed an elephant. This was our first duty to the video anyway. Leopards were fine if we could get a good sequence, but jumbos were primary.

We have seen several by this date, the eighteenth of October, but nothing like Hanley had inspected in his two safaris, the total of which ran to more than two hundred. But we kept looking, and added to those we had turned down by about eight. Each one we stalked, sometimes for a score of miles, sending the vehicle around to meet us and to keep a keen ear for a shot. I kept thinking of that big bugger we had seen on the first day of my safari, and he kept growing in size.

We stopped for lunch about at the perimeter of the rainfall, the earth smelling like Mother Russia in the spring. I passed up a herd of roan antelope (which were illegal, anyway) and also could have taken a fairly good gemsbok or oryx, but we were afraid of scaring away elephants. I hadn't fired a shot except at termite heaps, but I was sure hell on those! I was getting tired of cheese and macaroni, pork chops and beef, and I thought that an antelope would go nicely in the larder. But then I remembered that Volker gave all the meat to the Bushmen anyway. This seemed to be carrying diplomatic relations to a fault. . . .

One thing Bushmanland has is steinbok, antelope about the size of small dogs. They are everywhere, and it would be a rare day that we didn't see maybe twenty of them and a half-dozen duikers, larger but still smallish game. But I have never shot either a steinbok or a duiker. Neither did I shoot the diminutive dik-diks in Ethiopia. I suppose the trouble is that I have a pair of miniature pinschers, about five pounds apiece, who look exactly like steinbok. I have even promised to buy them horns and chin straps for Christmas.

Another species that occurs in unlimited numbers, rather like one of the biblical Egyptian plagues, is mice! There are a lot of hawks and eagles to keep them down, but if they were to try to tackle a population of rodents such as most of Namibia has, they would be so fat they couldn't get off the ground.

I first noticed this on the early safari with Mick Arsenault, when I was shooting (at) rock hyrax with Alex Butcher, another profesional hunter with Gary Haselau. Around a solitary water tank, there must have been untold thousands of them, which provided good shooting with Gary's old .22 Remington bolt-action rifle. They're harder to hit than you'd think at fifty yards!

Yet when we came to a dry draw or gulch below some promising cliffs, we saw even more. There were gymnogenes and other hawks ringing the place, but I'm sure they never made a dent in the population of mice, considering their few days of gestation. There were literally thousands, riffling the stunted grass and actually moving in waves! I suppose that mice go in cycles like lemmings, and that would account for the population unless there was some kind of underground water that attracted them.

They were also a major problem in stalking elephant in Bushmanland, since many places were undermined with mouse burrows that were more than noisy to step into, even if one didn't get a twisted ankle. The whole earth for dozens of acres was undercut, and, in the heat, most mice chose to stay underground, which worsened the problem.

After a couple of days I broke my own rule about hunting in low-cut desert shoes and barefoot in favor of ankle-length canvas boots and socks. For one thing, the ground was too hot at midday and through most of the afternoon not to wear socks, and the dirt that filtered into low-cuts from mouse tunnels was too much. Also, there were few grass seeds that time of year that

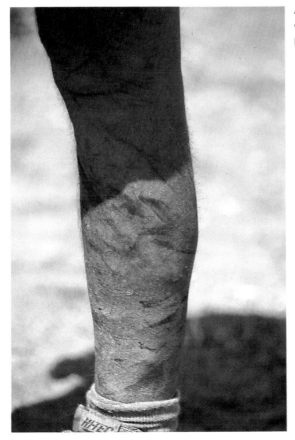

At the end of the season, walking is hard on the burned veld.

the mice hadn't already eaten, and they didn't get fouled with the socks as was usual in Botswana, Zimbabwe or Zambia.

After lunch we came to a small wallow that had remained undiscovered by Volker, and there had been elephants sloshing in it to coat themselves in mud to keep down temperatures and to repel insects. But there were no big tracks, at least nothing after the rain made everything a second set, as it had washed away all old spoor except what we found in cotton earth that was a foot deep from last year.

I was starting to get anxious. Would it rain tomorrow and put an end to the video? It looked fairly clear so far, but those damned clouds had a way of materializing that scared me. Both Phil and Roger had gotten some wonderful shots, but we didn't have an elephant on the ground yet, and time was getting relatively short.

On the return to camp, we found where another elephant had knocked down a leopard-bait tree, but the bait was untouched. I poured a cold beer and settled back while Fifi took a shower on return to camp. You don't really appreciate a fine camp unless you are whipped. The *en suite* showers were wonderful, and we could change in spacious privacy before meeting at the fire for one more of man's best friend before dinner. Volker and Anke knew how to do it right, that much is for sure.

With the crispness of newly ironed canvas shorts and a shirt, I felt like a new man. I had even run the electric razor across my bluish chops, while an appetite played jai alai in my belly.

Dinner was beefsteak, and it was beautifully done, T-bones cooked over the fire. Angi had even provided a choice of well-done (it *had* to be Fifi who chose the charred offerings) and rare, but with the luscious fat yellow and charred at the edges. But soon enough I was sleepy and we went to bed, the last notes of my harmonica shivering over the Kalahari sands. Sounds romantic. It was.

Dawn came just before five-thirty, but we were already up. Fifi had decided to stay back and try to compare the KwaNyama (the lingua franca of Ovamboland) with what she remembered when on border duty against Angola when she was a South African Defense Force linguist, spouting her ten languages, probably indiscriminately.

She had prepared a "briefing paper" for me to use while on safari and while writing this book, a 150-page document that really told the history and current status of the people of Namibia, then South-West Africa, as it was. I have often thought that she should write the books and I should do the research. . . .

Roger and Phil took their usual positions, and with Fifi at camp there was a bit more room topside with Johnny and Jonas. In a boil of dust, we left camp and picked up the Game Department man.

It was a few miles north of Tsumkwe that we hit a likely track. Even better, it followed the hunting "road" as we went along it for miles, finally breaking off to the left about fifteen miles west of the capital city. In referring to it as such, I have shown that I *do* have a sense of humor.

There were two bulls, the prints of both over twenty-four inches, and one looked to be about twenty-five inches, or a bit more than two of my boots. They were not loafing and rarely stopped to feed, but kept on to some sort of rendezvous of which only they knew. This brings up the point of communication among elephants.

The first elephant hunters thought that the low, throaty belly rumble of a bull and sometimes a cow elephant was strictly a digestive sound, which is not a poor conclusion, given the size of an elephant's stomach. Yet, even twenty years ago, I and others working with me thought that this was some kind of communication among herd members. In fact, I said so in various of my earlier writings. What really made me think that elephants could communicate was an experience I had while employed as a cropping officer by the government of Zambia. If a single animal escaped from our complete reduction of a herd of perhaps twenty or more, then we had at least a week of elephant problems such as their charging cars and assorted unseemly behavior. Obviously, the survivor was able to tell other elephants what had happened to itself and the family group. Those little hairless frogs again. . . .

That elephants can and do communicate on a level of "speech" below our threshold of hearing is beyond debate. As I recall, this was proved with zoo elephants in the northwest United States.

Exactly how far these lower-range transmissions can carry is not known, but the experience of scientists shows that the distance is considerable. Personally, I believe that the two elephant bulls we were tailing had been called by, and were in some sort of communication with, other elephant bulls. Well, the results show that I am correct.

We left the Toyota with water bags and all personnel. Roger made sure he was charged up, and Phil stripped in a new roll. From the time of the departure from the Toyota, we had, as usual, agreed on where everybody would stand if I got a shot. The idea was not to occlude anybody who had a camera.

I stuck two .470 Kynoch solid 500-grain rounds in the chambers of the Champlin-Famars and swung it shut like an airlock on a spaceship. Another two from the back of my cartridge holder went between my index and fourth fingers, the middle finger insulating them for easy and very quick reloading. I had a feeling that this might be "it." We began to walk.

The bulls were in a hurry, plowing through stuff that I thought they might stop to feed on. They did feed, but on the move. The sun positively scorched down, an incandescent ball that still had a few fingers of width to go before noon. We hadn't gone much more than a mile—and after a strong drink of water from the car's reservoir—when we were parched. All had a measured swig of the now-hot liquid, but I'll tell you, it tasted good!

The wind, which had been nearly dead, suddenly started to blow, but thank heaven it was from the spoor to us. I could even smell dung and the odor of zoos from the bulls, although they were far away.

We walked for perhaps six miles before a flagging ear brought us to a screeching stop in our tracks. Again, Volker had been right. The bulls were under a conglomeration of *lala* or vegetable ivory palms and still-green trees. But there were not two, there were ten! We stopped to measure them, and our position relative to them. The old taste of copper came up from my gullet and plated my tongue. I had the slight shakes of buck fever, but they soon went away, sort of. . . .

I was quite surprised to see by my watch, with its salt-caked band, that it was a few minutes after two in the afternoon. I had thought it much earlier.

Carefully measuring the wind, we glassed the bulls as best we could. After this, I was certain that I wanted one particular one that would go into the eighties, a monster that was directly behind a bush, showing only the top of his massive back and his tusks at a hundred yards.

The bulls were standing in two clumps, three at the far left and seven under some fairly shady trees. The one I wanted was with the seven, and I decided then that he was mine.

We backed off twenty or so yards, more for our own psychology than for fear that the elephants would hear our whispered urgencies.

I wanted to ease in, give a side-brain shot to the big chap and then cut the wind as all hell broke loose from the other nine. But, as Volker wisely pointed out, it would be dangerous to get Phil as well as Roger and himself into such a tricky position with at least six other elephants that might do the unexpected. Like eat us. . . .

He was right of course. It was a fine one-man show, but it was impossible to pull off without considerable risk of life. We could not even defend ourselves by having to shoot. The Game Department would ask what in hell we were doing pressuring those elephants in the first place, when there could be a multiple charge. I did not much fancy one of those nice, snug Namibian jail cells, with the election a couple of weeks off. So we decided we would wait until the ten started moving at something after five o'clock.

I thought my watch had stopped, so slowly did the three hours go. I sat. I squatted. I knelt, every second that elephant getting bigger and harder to hit properly. I even tried sitting, my knees to my chin. Time went no faster. I decided that the seconds were as overheated as I was, and that was why they moved so slowly.

It was almost four o'clock now, and I was kneeling on one knee, the .470 having had its cartridges changed for cool ones as many times as Phil had checked over his camera, which was plenty. Maybe the heat was getting to me, but I suddenly flashed back to Marlin Perkins's "Wild Kingdom" and whispered to Phil, "Gee, Marlin, there's a whole passel of 'em over here!"

Phil picked up the drift. "Why, you're right, Jim! Let's get closer and see how they protect their families from harm with Mutual of Omaha. Like disappearing up their own pink arse-holes!"

I smothered a chuckle under Volker's stern gaze. Of course, he wouldn't understand, not being an American raised on TV.

The minutes continued to drone by, interrupted by flies attracted by the elephants' *marfi*—better said, droppings. It was just as well that we were a good distance away, as we had to give the Australian national salute many times to keep the pests off our faces. One even kamikazed my eye, but I fished him out, bedraggled but none the worse for wear considering what was to come for him.

The elephants seemed not to have moved a whisker, simply swaying back and forth as they semi-slept the white, hot afternoon away. Even the sky was almost bleached, no longer the fine, new blue denim of the morning. Through my glasses I continued to watch the elephants.

For sure, from what I could see, the big chap on the far right was my choice. It was hard to tell what he went, weight-wise, on the tusks, but I thought he was eighty pounds at a minimum. He was huge in body size, but even for that his tusks seemed big—great dirty-white parentheses that were sap- and dirt-stained from maybe approaching a half-century of rooting and tree-smashing. He had fought with them, too, as they showed old signs of his having sharpened them. Oh, yes, elephants *do* sharpen their tusks. I have never seen this, but Dr. Anthony Hall-Martin, one of the top experts in the world on elephants, has witnessed it. In fact, Anthony claims that fighting between bulls is the largest cause of death among sexually active elephants. And he ought to know; he is in charge of all the elephants in South Africa's Kruger National Park, a showcase of sound elephant management.

At a quarter to five, there were a few ear flaps waving, which showed that maybe the herd was ready to move. There was also a slight shifting of massive bodies as the sun canted lower and some color returned to the sky, a rosy flush starting to bleed all over the west. Something was going to happen pretty soon, I thought, and eased up into a standing position, checked the .470, and put the glasses back on the two segments of the herd, swinging between them.

I looked at Roger, and he gave me a thumbs-up signal, swinging the Betacam to his shoulder. Phil did the same with the Nikon. The trackers as well as the Game Department man would stay behind, but I admonished them not to stay too far behind, as there was no telling how the bulls would break from their pod once the shooting started.

At almost the stroke of five, the three bulls in the separate group started to come over to the seven. We started to move, the buck fever strangely gone, although it had been nineteen years since I had looked at a jumbo over the rib of a rifle.

As we eased nearer the herd, my mind began to flood with memories, as in a very bad movie. I remembered the first bull with Antonio, the Italian. The days of blood and terror, cropping the excess of the herds. I remembered the time Silent saved my life by throwing a water bag into the face of a wounded bull after bad (Bad? Almost terminal) bullet performance with a .458 Magnum. I remembered the shots I had to make when clients drew a charge with a poor placement of their bullets. I remembered the big fellow that I frontally brain-shot at five yards with the old .375 before it could quite reach me with outstretched trunk. I also remembered Katwindwi, pinned to the stony earth with a single tusk, and the last drink of water I gave him before he died in growing agony as the shock wore off. I remembered Denton-Smythe and his crumpled, blanket-wrapped form in the rear of that Land-Rover so many years ago—so smashed and crushed by a herd that I didn't know which end was the head. Yes, I remembered.

There were also the good times to remember. There were Rudy Cabañas's two big bulls; the day Bobby Welch killed a fine one right in front of a deep cut in Botswana's Okavango. There was also the bullfighter and the doctors and the lawyers and many, many fine elephants. But this was not today, I realized. Today was something special: my own elephant and the battle with my own mortality. . . .

Volker looked over his shoulder, and I took the lead. God-damn the mice! I sank up to my ankles noisily with each step taken in a low crouch as the elephants got bigger. The thought flitted through my mind that there could be nothing to the old tale that jumbos were afraid of mice! Hell, they'd be paranoid here! Ahead, I could see the group of bulls moving, swinging slowly to my right. Then they stopped and went to the left! What had happened? Had they changed their minds, or possibly caught a tiny sound or a whiff of wind? As I turned after them, all thoughts were very unprofessionally gone as to where Phil, Roger and Volker were. It was now me and the elephant. Hey! Now they were going straight away!

I swung in a parallel position as the big bulls showed us their sterns, baggy, gray things that looked like huge, soiled pajamas.

The smell of elephant, crushed, dry grass and dung was strong in my nostrils as I closed with a burst to forty yards, just as the huge fellow cut left and put a pal between us. They were playing three-dimensional chess with us! A couple of times I even half-raised the .470 Nitro for a shot, but the gap quickly closed between bulls. Beneath our feet, I could hear the dry crumbling as the mouse runways crushed under our weight. Man, but it was hard going, like one of those nightmares in which you can't run as a huge and ugly creature bears down to take you to feed to its young.

I have to hand it to Phil and Roger—they stayed with me, as did Volker. I wanted to dash in and cool the big chap with a brain shot, but realized that the cameras could never keep up with me. It was a curious problem: no video shots, no commercial production. But, maybe, with video shots there would be no elephant. . . .

We had covered only a hundred yards with the twisting and turning of the herd, but with the mouse tunnels it seemed miles. The big bull with those lovely teeth was now on the other side of the herd and gaining distance fast. Something would have to be done.

I felt Volker's hand grab my shoulder like a gorilla instructing its young. He physically turned me to the left and said in a rasping whisper, "Shoot that one! The big one there!" It only took nanoseconds to register, and the .470 came up, the rib of the barrels sheeting heat between a shimmering, retreating form of a bull elephant.

Automatically, the ivory bead nestled in the notch of the rear express sights and stayed there. The first shot was over a piece of deadwood, a raking 500-grain solid that entered the lower flank and knifed forward through the vital organs, destined for the heart. I was unaware of the muzzle blast and the recoil, only that the bull elephant disappeared from view in recoil as seventy-five grains of cordite equivalent slammed me back and shifted my field of view. But it had seemed a good shot, and I tore the skyward express down from the recoil and saw that the bull had veered to the left, giving me a better angle. I touched the second barrel off with a lead of perhaps two feet on the lower shoulder-heart area and clearly heard the bullet thump, this time at about eighty yards. I pinged the empty casings over my shoulder and reloaded, dropping two of the brass bananas down the twin tubes of the chambers. I raised the rifle again, the heat mirage even stronger from the friction of the first two shots.

I knew one thing from the hundreds I had shot cropping and on safari: he was mine. I saw both puffs of dust from the bull's hide as the big solids struck, and knew that I had probably hit him in the heart both times. From the impact against dried wallow mud, the bullets were like tracers or spotter rounds. But what if I was wrong? What if the bull continued to go, through

The herd containing the author's elephant.

bone deflection or such? What if they were bad bullets? All we needed was a wounded elephant, the first in my career that would need following up. So I shot him twice again.

The third shot was again right on the money at about ninety yards, and the fourth likewise at about a hundred yards. This is a long way for a shot at an elephant, and I favored the frontal or angled brain shot above all others, but there was no time to deliver it, given distances involved and change of angles. I had only a heart shot open, so I took it. It wasn't what I wanted for the video, but it was my only choice. That, or go without an elephant. . . .

As it was, it was not even the elephant I had chosen, but Volker was right that I had to take the second bull, which was closer. He could see the cameramen, and I couldn't. His choice was correct.

There was a relatively open area between where the elephants had spent the afternoon and the next piece of lowish cover. I was prepared to wait for the bull to drop, but I was as nervous as a chicken having lunch at Colonel Sanders when the bull finally came to a stop and breathed his last. Slowly, at 120 yards, he crumpled as he would in a classic heart shot when the oxygen ran out for his brain. He swayed and then crashed in a welter of dust and hot dirt, but he died better than he would have when he used the last of his teeth, and they were already worn and slick. He was old. Very old.

I believe in paying the insurance, so I shot him again in the heart at forty yards and then approached him to make sure he was gone. He was.

I walked around him, marveling that he had not died of old age with his massive temple dents, as big as soup tureens, and his almost slick oval rear feet. He had any number of strange lumps and healed scars, his ears as tattered as the sails of a ghost ship. His eyes were rheumy, and above all, his tail was almost bare, just a few short hairs embedded in it, as compared to the flowing glory of a bull in his prime. He was not old; he was ancient. A strange thought came to mind: we were born at about the same time.

I had forgotten, but for Volker's prompting, that this was the bull that had reached into his forward stomach with his trunk and covered himself with a cool burst of water and partially digested matter. The heat must have been too much for him, so he cooled down.

He was mine. Not that I really owned him, but he was my partner forever in a great adventure. His tusks would always remind me of the day I shot my own elephant, and nobody could ever take that away. Granted, it went quite a bit harder with him than with me, but he was in for a terrible, lingering death anyway. If I were given a choice—not that he was—I would have taken the bullet, neat and sweet. But I did not kill him because he would die anyway, I killed him because for a moment we

The author with his elephant.

were one. I doubt that you who have not hunted and killed big game will see my point, but those of you who have, well, you know. . . . Is this a weak explanation? Perhaps, but I think not. Had he killed me or Volker or Phil or Roger, it would have been the same.

There was no doubt that his ivory was good—excellent, in fact. His right tusk had driven into the ground as he fell dead, but it was immediately exhumed by anxious trackers. I guessed him in the seventy-pound range, as did Volker, and we were spot-on. He went a hair over that mark for the larger tusk and a couple of pounds under for the working tusk, being right-handed—or right-tusked—as most are.

No, I didn't kill the one that was bigger than this, but given the circumstances, I was very happy. There was no way to get the big one and get pictures, too, and when Volker told me to shoot the smaller one, he was right, and protesteth too much I do not.

It was almost dark when we returned to the hunting car, about four miles away. I was whipped with mental exhaustion, but I felt good. At last it was over, and I had not screwed it up. The elephant was dead as neatly as circumstances would permit, and nobody had been hurt. The video was in the can or cassette, and Phil was happy with what he had gotten on his Nikon.

I had hoped for a brain shot, as Phil had much experience of elephants and had photographed them for more than twenty-five years, including every natural circumstance they could be found in, including moonlight and bush fires. He was quite leery of coming with me to *hunt* an elephant, but he realized that he had better see all phases of elephants before he could later devote himself to their study, as he has done.

CHAPTER

TEN

Itook the elephant's tail, in what may possibly be one of the oldest hunting ceremonies that determine ownership of a carcass. It was now in the Toyota with me.

It was well after dark when we bumped and rolled into the camp at Klein Dobe, where Fifi and the rest of the people were waiting. I was curiously subdued until I saw how well the video had turned out, and then I was ecstatic. It was good, as you will see if you happen to buy one. Roger had done a first-class job, and I thought Phil had done the same, but we would have to wait until processing back in Arizona, where he lived, to see for sure. Dinner was put off for several hours as we told our tale and celebrated the death of a fine old bull, not his demise.

The next morning we went back to the dead bull and found it untouched by hyenas or anything else. Arriving just after sunrise, we saw the Department of Conservation trucks pull in with scores of hungry Ju/Wasi Bushmen, who cut it up along lines drawn in chalk by Arnold. Volker and I did some stuff for the video, and then stood by to watch the proceedings.

There is nothing delicate about rendering a bull elephant, and I had seen it untold times before. Shortly there was a strong fire burning and the first strips of the backstrap, which had lovely fat attached, were thrown into the flames to cook—or scorch—Bushman-style. It was stirred about a bit by the killing spears, and was actually medium by the time it was fished out.

The older men had first go, and I entered their circle and gestured that I would like some, too. One man, who features prominently in the video, was probably fresh from a drinking bout as he gesticulated not bad-humoredly with a large, white-handled machete with which he was cutting off mouthfuls some-

In this feeding frenzy of elephant meat, that panga is a bit too close and the author's smile is artificial. Possibly the gentleman had some beer before coming to the dinner party. Or perhaps he just doesn't like Irishmen.

how without taking his nose with them. Heaven knows, he was enjoying it.

I was handed a piece that the man had been chewing on, and I tried my best to cut it properly, but I was chicken and cut off a chunk that would barely fit into my mouth. Somehow I was able to engulf it, and I tell you that it was delicious. It tasted

The author managed to cut off a piece of fire-done elephant filet without slicing off his nose, which is rather prominent.

like the best charcoaled steak and had beautiful fat that I was unaware an elephant had on its backstraps. My later regret was that I had taken none back to camp, as I'm sure it would not have been missed by the Ju/Wasi.

I returned to the Toyota and saw that the head had been severed at the neck and loaded into the back. The tusks would be removed back in camp. This was better than taking them out

194

The author's knife appears to have impressed the Bushman. It certainly got his attention!

here, as there would be more time at Klein Dobe. There would be no time to bury the skull for a week or so, because my trip would be over too soon. The ivory would accumulate some small nicks in the chopping-out process, but you can bet your patootie that I had arranged with Volker that Fifi and I would take the tusks back with us to South Africa, rather than leave them to the discretion of a new government!

While the bull was being butchered, two of my .470 solid bullets were returned to me. I had no idea how many there were, or whether some had gone right through the body of the tusker. He had fallen on his right side, whereas I had shot him on the left. This is unusual; normally they tend to fall on the same side they are shot on, for some reason. In case of a brain shot, they often fall in a kneeling position, balanced on folded legs. In fact, Ken Wilson edited into the tape a pair of brain shots that had taken place in Tanzania. They are absolutely spectacular.

I took quite a few trophies from the bull, as this was probably the last one I would kill. Also, there were leopard baits to think of; we had no meat in camp besides groceries, and there will be a snowball fight in Hades before I use a roast beef as bait!

There were all four lower legs and feet, a great deal of skin, and, of course, the ivory. I also took the tail. Waste not, want not. But I can tell you that in six hours or so there was nothing on the ground where that elephant lay but a slight greasy spot. The Bushmen took *everything*—bowels, organs, skin, meat and all except the stomach contents. They even took the bones, but dug a shallow hole for the undigested fodder. I even saw some of them wringing the offal out with a grimy fist and letting the moisture flow into their mouths. Nothing finicky about the Ju/ Wasi. . . .

Although I did not see them leave, I saw the place a few days later and learned at the time that meat was being taken as far as two hundred miles away, to Western Bushmanland, which has almost no water but it does have a few Bushmen. Possibly this transportation of meat was the equivalent of the "gift ring"

A .458 Winchester Magnum bullet flanked by two .470 solids that were recovered from the author's elephant.

of artifacts. All shared in the meat, no matter who cut it, behavior that does not exist among the black Bantu.

On the way home, we made a deviation to check a few of the old leopard baits, but nothing had fed. We hadn't done the usual ten or twenty miles of walking, spooring elephant, and I was secretly glad that it was not necessary. I was beat, mentally and physically, and we had the tape we needed. I told Roger that

197

if he let anybody get near that material with even a weak magnet, I would very happily kill him slowly, even though his wife had given birth to a child while he was grafting in Bushmanland. I'm not sure he didn't think I meant it. . . . Well, maybe I did.

We arrived back in camp at about five o'clock, a leisurely afternoon, and I decided that we would not go out again. Screw leopards. Let's work with the cameras and such. I promptly took a nap.

It was still light when I awoke ten minutes later. Perhaps I felt guilty. But what had actually awakened me was the knowledge that there was a cutter termite hole not far away, and it would make excellent footage. We shot most of a cassette of these fascinating creatures, but, like Edgar the Chameleon, there was no space for it in the video.

Cutter termites will defoliate an entire couple of acres of dead grass, sticks, or, from what I can gather, anything that is made of cellulose. These termites do not build hills or heaps, but usually have a simple hole in the ground into which there is a constant flow of this stuff. I have watched for hours as a worker arrived with too big a stick to get down the hole and tried interminably (no pun meant) to make it fit. The worker is harassed for his capitalistic ideas, but eventually gets it down the hole, which is about a half-inch across.

Some of these termites actually farm the processed cellulose and grow mushrooms on it, but this is beyond my ability and experience as an entomologist. These creatures are truly a captivating microcosm of life in New York, which I *do* know.

Now that I was up, it was time to relax around the fire, and we all did so in great fashion. When it comes to relaxing, I have gained a professional status, and Fifi is a senior amateur.

Doug agreed to hang the fresh elephant knuckles as bait the next day while we stayed in camp and got a few static shots we needed. One was that I had to trephine an elephant skull and explain to the Betacam where the brain was and at what proper angle it could be reached by a bullet.

For this demonstration we chose a sixty-pounder that had been taken early in the season. Working with the bare bone of

No food is wasted from an elephant; this is shade-dried biltong.

the skull after reinserting the tusks in their sockets, I used a hardwood pointer to show where the eye, the ear hole, and the brain cavity were once the skull was chain-sawed in half longitudinally.

A brain shot is tough; most tries are too high. I hope that Ken Wilson's Tanzanian shots in the video, combined with this demonstration, will help.

We spent the day of October 20, after lunch, working with Bushmen and shooting some angles of the camp, but mostly we goofed off. The next day we would have to make hay if we were to do the leopard tape as well as the elephant piece.

We decided that in the morning Volker and I and perhaps Fifi would check leopard baits while we sent Roger and Phil north to the Kaudom Reserve to film some female and young elephants. We had no idea whether there would be any or not, but there was plenty of spoor, so they took a lunch with Arnie and left well before dawn.

This, incidentally, was the morning that we later found the puff adder behind the wastebasket. Damned lucky that nobody blundered into it in the predawn murk!

After checking the leopard baits, and determining that the dog and heifer killer had not come back near the village since his fright that full-moon night, we decided to sit the next one along, the one that had the open space in front of it. We had no cameras, but maybe we could slip in and at least get a leopard, since I had pretty well given up the idea of the video. It looked as if it just wouldn't work out.

Volker and I fried from about three o'clock until late dusk, but there was never a show by the male leopard. We had hoped that, since he was feeding regularly, he might come in behind the bait, but he was a no-show.

We were in little humor for jokes, and had just grabbed a beer each when Roger and Phil came back from the showers. They had seen nothing either, they said; the Kaudom was strangely dead. So it was a wasted day, which did little to raise our spirits. Before dinner, Phil and Roger casually mentioned that we had better review some tape on the small monitor and see what we still needed. They had already set things up in the dining hut.

Volker and I were still stewing, but a bit more mellow, when the tape began to roll. I did a double-take. So did Volker. There were four cassettes of elephants, doing whatever elephants do in their vast repertoire of activities. They had put us on, having found several large herds of females and young that had come down to drink and wallow in the water and mud of a water hole. The day was not wasted—far from it—and I was delighted as soon as I got over my most ungracious slump in good humor. Phil told us that he had even taken all the film he had except for the one in one of his camera bodies, held in reserve just in case.

I was anxious about the ivory of my elephant, and asked Volker when we could get some videos and stills of it being chopped out. He thought that the next day would be fine. In the morning we took a run for a big kudu, but saw none except a few females, and returned to camp about ten. Mateus, an Angolan refugee who worked in the kitchen, and Jonas were the tusk-removal specialists, and they were already well on their way, a pile of meat that they had pared away growing next to the skull. No meat of any kind ever went to waste.

I narrated the ivory-removal process for the camera, and at last the ivory was free of its bone sockets. The men had done a good job, too, only a very few marks showing from their pangas.

At this point the important thing was the nerve. If it was a large one, as long as most that we had seen removed in Bushmanland, there would be considerable space that might otherwise have been occupied by ivory taken up by the conical pulp. There was no way to tell whether an elephant had a large nerve pulp or not, since it was not visible until it was removed. Still, I was heartened as Jerry Heiner's bull had pulps a full thirty-four inches long and still was well over eighty pounds per side— really exceptional. If the nerves had been smaller, the bull might conceivably have weighed close to ninety pounds. I was quite nervous when the time came to pull the pulp.

It is an interesting thing that among most black tribes there is one or another chunk of magic attached to nerve removal. In many tribes, only an old man may take them out with impunity, all others, especially young men and women, supposedly becoming sterile if they witness their removal. Perhaps what we need in Africa is more public nerve-pulling, if there is the slightest shred of truth in the legend. . . .

At last the moment arrived, and Jonas began to ease out the nerve with a steel sharpening stick. When he was finished, I was very pleased. The pulp was only eighteen inches long, which would add considerable weight to the tusks, perhaps as much as four pounds each.

On the scales, the larger tusk just made seventy, and the working or right tusk was sixty-eight pounds, a very fine elephant, to be sure, but I couldn't help wondering what my choice from that bull herd, probably now grazing not fifty miles away, would have weighed.

I wanted some close-ups of the nerves for this book, so Doug Stephensen stuck around with Phil while we examined them. Suddenly I noted a hard object at the tip of one of the nerves, and wondered what in hell it could be. It turned out to be the very rare pearl or seed ivory, and the lump I felt was not alone! There were thirteen pearls, including a very rare double that was attached to another fairly big one, literally worth a fortune in the East, especially in Sri Lanka, formerly Ceylon. I had only seen one instance of these before, from Kenya, when somebody I knew had a few strung and made into a bracelet for his baby daughter.

When I got home, I started to research these rare ivory globules, found entirely free-floating in the nerve pulp. There was very, very little in my considerable library of things elephantine—in fact, a flat nothing in over a hundred works on elephants alone. So the logical approach was to send one to Anthony Hall-Martin in the hope that he could help me solve the mystery of their formation.

Anthony was back to me shortly, and enclosed several copied pages from Dr. Sylvia Sykes's excellent book, *The Natural*

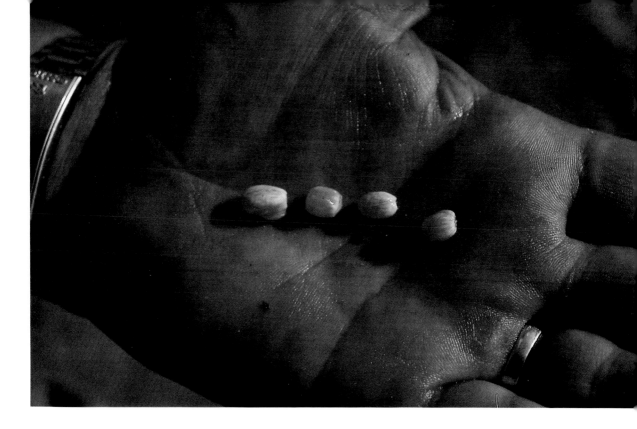

History of the African Elephant (London: Weidenfeld and Nich-olson, 1971), which seemed to deal with the matter of seed ivory. There was one reference to pearl ivory from a bull that Dr. Sykes (quite a gal, apparently) shot in 1965 at Ndi, Kenya. Sykes says that the bull had one normal tusk and one very abnormal right tusk, which had several supernumerary tusklets and was filled with pus, as well as having some pearl ivory in the pulp itself. The material is described as "reactionary dentine" and usually occurs attached to the tusk itself. This is the only reference to pearl ivory that I can find as free-floating material, although by such a term I mean not attached to the tusk but free internally in the pulp cavity.

It is interesting that other cases mentioned by Sykes are all attached to a tusk and caused by disease, whereas in my elephant there was absolutely no sign of disease, old or recent.

Therefore, I suspect that there is no *known* cause of pearl or seed ivory but disease, but it would seem that extreme age

203

can also possibly be a causal factor. I really don't know, but I can say one thing: I must learn to speak in italics so that scientists can understand me when I say such things as, "Excuse me, but your semicolon is showing."

Ivory is very interesting stuff, and deserves a word here, although I will try not to step on my own toes with material found in former books I have midwifed.

You don't need to be told that it has been a gauge of wealth since the days of early "madonnas" carved of mammoth teeth back in the Aurignacian period, maybe earlier. That it is a classic store of wealth today is obvious also from the hammering that elephants are getting. Perhaps it is valued because of its natural characteristics, as it is only dentine as found in human teeth, but distributed a bit more liberally to an elephant.

A piece I read the other day in a British journal suggests that all our problems are over, since a powder has been developed that when compressed and mixed, becomes a fair substitute for ivory. This idea, naturally, is parallel to tying certain patterns of salmon-fishing flies with plastic jungle cock imitation, since in somebody's wisdom the "enameled" neck feathers or hackles of the Indian bird are now prohibited to import because the bird is endangered. Since the jungle cock, the ancestor of the domestic chicken, has achieved such an elevated status, those whole and preserved necks that are still available have sextupled and more in value. Supply and demand. Of course, the average Atlantic salmon wouldn't know a plastic "feather" from a garbage truck or a dangling participle, but if you're going to tie "correct" salmon flies, you must use the "eyed" feathers of a jungle cock. Flies are tied for fishermen, anyway, not salmon.

Ivory is prized by pool players—although most billiard and pool cue balls are made today from good plastics—because of its beauty. Concert pianists prefer it because it tends to absorb the slight perspiration that accumulates on the keys, and bagpipe makers use it for joints in their "doodlesacks" because a bagpipe is made with ivory joints and that's that. Ivory is cool to the hand, whereas plastic takes on ambient heat. About ten years ago I had a Colt .45 Combat Commander restocked with ivory grips after using rubber or checkered walnut wood for quite a while. What a difference! I first thought it would be fairly slippery, but it gives a grip like a Samurai sword. Every shooter at my local gun club was amazed, and I soon became the first kid on the block to be elected president.

Ivory is unmistakable, probably because it is an animal substance. It grips well, takes on a superb patina with age, and is easily workable as it is relatively soft. When Rob Charlton, the owner of Damascus USA, which probably makes the finest forged Damascus blades in the world, came out with the Cap-

Elephant hide, Charlton Damascus Capstick African knife, and two .470 Nitro Express cartridges.

stick African, a design that was Rob's but that I liked very much, he supplied me with serial number 000, hilted with elephant ivory. Now, *there* is a knife!

The beauty of ivory, whether it comes from elephant, walrus, narwhal, sperm whale or hippo, is that it is cross-hatched with a semitranslucent pattern depending upon what blank is used. The single finest piece I ever saw, I bought when I was still at the University of Virginia for sixty dollars (no, we had stopped using Confederate money) as grips for a single-action six-shooter I had. It was made of mammoth ivory, dug out of some Siberian or Alaskan permafrost, and it had the finest and boldest grain imaginable. I sold it, and the revolver and belt and three boxes of ammo, for the same sixty dollars about a year later. Seems I was in love again, or something. Lord, send me a callow, untried youth who wants to sell his mammoth-ivory six-gun. . . .

There is not really a point in listing how much ivory has been stockpiled and traded, sold at warehouses from Mombasa to London to New York. There are plenty of books that will do that for you. The point is that ivory has always been popular. But then, there's ivory and there's (you guessed it) ivory.

Considered the best stuff is the eastern African substance, including the "rose" ivory of Congo, which may be largely that of the Forest Elephant, *Loxodonta cyclotis*. I have seen quite a bit of it during a lifetime, but damn me if I see any rose coloring to it. Maybe it gets its reputation from the fact that it is exceptionally soft and that those beautiful roses or concentric Chinese balls can be carved from it. I really don't know.

As I have said before, the usual trade route was that of black ivory, the circuit practiced by the Arabs, mostly. A caravan or *safari* used newly captured or bought slaves to carry the ivory back to the coast from whence it usually found its way back to Zanzibar, which was the hub of most slaving activity in eastern Africa.

In fact, some of the ivory/slave traders such as Tippoo Tib (so named for the sound of a firing rifle and a ricocheting bullet) really saved Stanley and Emin Pasha, despite his objectionable life-style. Ivory-hilted knives and forks from Sheffield, as well as pianos and drawing-room fixtures, played a major role in opening Africa.

But, why does ivory continue as the premier substance? Simple. Despite the imitations nothing even comes close. Ivory is ivory, the real stuff, and elephants grow the best.

Perhaps a parallel may be drawn with pearls. The imitations, made from one sort of plastic or polished, compressed bone meal are still imitations. Unlike ivory, it is sometimes difficult to tell the difference between the real thing and imitations. Perhaps the advice I am about to give you is worth more than the price of this book. A real pearl can be detected by rubbing it across one's front teeth edges. If it is rough and catches the enamel, then it is real. If it is slippery and slick, it is no pearl. It is a form of plastic. Hydrocarbons tell all.

I have come across at least one interesting item since the last time I wrote about ivory. Sylvia Sykes notes that ivory powder has long been considered a panacea for various diseases, so she decided, in a controlled experiment, to try some mixed with dirt for her geraniums. The geraniums died.

Yet, in another experiment, not by Sykes, roses flourished with an addition of ivory powder. Who knows?

CHAPTER
ELEVEN

I heard from Hanley Sayers in November in a fax in which he told me that it looked pretty dismal that he would ever get his tusks from that magnificent 94-pounder. I was heartsick for him as I know that was the greatest trophy of his life. He had made the mistake I dared not make, leaving the ivory behind with legislation and a Marxist government coming in under Sam Nujoma, who won the election. Because the Americans supported anti-communist forces in Angola, the Marxists were not especially pro-Yankee and maybe this had something to do with the fact that Hanley's tusks were not forthcoming.

But, the above paragraph made me think to call Volker Grellmann to find out the status of the ivory and he assures me that the only hold-up has been that Namibia has not joined CITES since it became independent from South Africa. The process of joining is coming along well and it looks after all as if Hanley will get his tusks. I am most happy for him. He earned them.

It was more than hot now, the searing heat even continuing at night as we lay on sopped mattresses and punctuated our rollings with coolish showers and damp towels. I was taking six salt tablets a day, as was Fifi. Leopards knew better than to feed in the heat of even early mornings and we never even saw one let alone had a shot since Jerry Heiner collected his so easily.

Even the bush was so dry that a short walk caused quite a bit of bleeding and a constant marking on my legs from naturally caused fires. I had, in fact, started to wonder if the fire that had so nearly fried the camp was not set by somebody. The wind was just right and it seemed to start from the downwind side of a small path that crossed camp about three-quarters of a mile in front. It seems very unlikely that the Bushmen would want to burn us out, as they got any amount of meat from us. But, it was an awfully convenient place to break out into flames. . . .

At last, the 29th of October arrived, the day we were supposed to leave for Windhoek. I say "at last" not because the trip was unsuccessful or in any way unpleasant, but after all, Phil and I had been there for about six weeks and Roger even longer. In fact, Roger could have filed for citizenship, but he seemed to like that blue passport with gold lettering. I don't blame him.

Phil and Volker had left the morning before with Roger's virtual tons of video gear in one of the four-wheel-drive cars and that left Fifi, Roger, and myself to fly back with an Israeli pilot whom Fifi absolutely stunned by saying in Hebrew: "Good-bye. Thanks very much. It was a very pleasant flight." The pilot goggled in disbelief and answered her only in English. "Where did you learn to say that? You're not Jewish, are you?"

"Ah, it's a very long time ago. You know that Israel and South Africa used to be very close? Well, I spent some time on a *moshav*. No, I'm not Jewish, but I like your country."

We left Bushmanland at about seven in the morning and arrived at Eros—nothing erotic about it—Airport about midmorning. We had been seen off by Johnny, Jonas, and all the rest of the safari crew, and I had the feeling that even had I not distributed largesse rather liberally, they still would have been there.

I would like to say that the country turned greener the closer we came to Windhoek, but if anything, this land between two deserts looks like both of them. On the way from the airport to Volker and Anke's home, I was astonished at the building boom that was going on. The city had mushroomed even while we were away in Bushmanland. New embassies, I guess, now that Namibia was at the beginning of having its own government under the South West African People's Organization. I suppose the theory was that at least they know where the communists stand, or think they do.

Volker picked us up and we went to his home for the packaging of the tusks in bubble plastic and burlap. We learned one really funny thing there: Phil had shared his newly made bed, crisp sheets and all, with a small scorpion that had proceeded to sting him, as I recall, where he is biggest. We had gone the entire time in Bushmanland without a threat of a scorpion except for their residences in dead wood and such, only to have Phil hit in a proper bed under the most unlikely of circumstances!

Volker and Anke have a large office attached to their house that acts as the pivotal point of their safaris. The tusks were not there yet, and I started to worry unnecessarily. Soon they were, looking like a couple of small bodies that were then wrapped completely in impact-resistant material. I thought we might be in for a few adventures carrying these through two lots of customs people who even if they had not read the articles on the supposed perfidy of hunters, they at least looked at the pictures.

There was a considerable amount of overweight payable, given Roger's video stuff and the tusks, but we were glad to pay it rather than to start some confrontation with an official who needed to be noticed. Documentation was excellent and I found myself a little bit disappointed that we had not been asked for it. For sure, our papers would be scrutinized when we entered South Africa.

Volker helped us a lot and we had said good-bye to Anke at her home. Soon we were seated and the South African Airways jet took off. This service was by Airbus, but we had been lucky to get a 747 for the relatively short hop on the way up.

I have had a year since we returned, to monitor the situation and to watch new developments in the elephant crisis, as much as I hate to use the word but it is accurate because, after all, elephants are being murdered for financial gain.

Certainly, as important if not more so than conservation is the use of armed personnel to combat even better armed poachers. This has worked very well in Kenya, Tanzania, and Zimbabwe. Botswana doesn't seem to have gotten the word, perhaps because its geographical harshness and vastness doesn't lend itself to poachers' operations the way that those countries more closely located to "clearing" areas do. A truck found carrying $2,000,000 (*dollars!*) worth of ivory and rhino horn saw its owner fined a very ineffectual $2,600 in 1989. Obviously, courts so disposed enhance rather than reduce poaching.

Of course, the guilt lies much more with the "middleman" or the organizer of shipments of ivory as one can't really blame a peasant in the bush for realizing how his deeds affect populations of pachyderms, which includes rhinos. He sees several years income in taking a single or perhaps two elephants which bring hundreds of times his fee when utilized by the end-user. Yet, the bush dweller is the guy who gets shot by anti-poaching patrols. His activities get the most florid press treatment: tusks are "ripped" and "torn" from the dead elephants, not carefully chopped out to give the ivory the highest value. Oh, well, what's the harm of a little purple passion by the press?

The real turnabout will come when the people really responsible for an ivory crisis are punished in the first place. For example, Burundi has for years been a major exporter of ivory. But, they have no elephants of their own. It hardly takes a Rhodes scholar to figure out that something is amiss. It used to be the policy of the Kenya conservation forces that poaching by personnel of the force itself was not investigated despite the mounds of carcasses quite near the camps themselves.

Ideally, the optimum situation would be that of no appreciable poaching; some cropping from a healthy overpopulation of elephants by responsible governments; an appreciable education of rural Africans to the worth of the elephant and other big game as a value "on the ground" to them, not somebody else, far away; and carefully controlled sport hunting permitting, through fees, licenses, taxes, and such, the monetary wherewithal to make the above ideas possible.

What it really comes down to is a collusion, even if artificial, between supply and demand. There are only so many elephants, less every year now that legal hunting has stopped in many areas. It is relatively simple to establish a "world price" of a grade of ivory if it is cleared through a central and *non-corrupt* body that must be created. The answer is not *no* trade, because the commodity loses value if it is prohibited from trade. And, the commodity's greatest value, curiously enough, if properly managed, should be the prevention of illegal killing of elephants and the salvation of the species.

It is further essential that *sport hunted* ivory be completely removed from the *commercial market* so that it doesn't muddy the water internationally. It should be simple enough to note what is sport hunted and what is not.

There is really no reason to stop trade in such an ancient commodity. The idea is to stop illegality. The ivory trade ban as instituted by voters of last year at the CITES conference is as unrealistic as the Volstead Act. Where there is a demand, you can count on it that there will be supply and there will be as long as there are *any* elephants.

What is the answer? Make elephants so valuable on the ground to local people that they will make money legitimately if utilized and lose it if elephants and other game are poached. See then how many "informers" there are against poachers, middlemen, and end users. Only if elephants are worth more to the people who share a territory with them than a poacher will receive for their ivory will elephants and rhinos be truly safe.